T0185496

Learn Windows Subsystem for Linux

A Practical Guide for Developers and IT Professionals

Prateek Singh

Apress®

Learn Windows Subsystem for Linux: A Practical Guide for Developers and IT Professionals

Prateek Singh
Bangalore, India

ISBN-13 (pbk): 978-1-4842-6037-1   ISBN-13 (electronic): 978-1-4842-6038-8
https://doi.org/10.1007/978-1-4842-6038-8

Managing Director, Apress Media LLC: Welmoed Spahr
Acquisitions Editor: Louise Corrigan
Development Editor: James Markham
Coordinating Editor: Nancy Chen

Cover designed by eStudioCalamar

Cover image designed by Freepik (www.freepik.com)

Distributed to the book trade worldwide by Springer Science+Business Media New York, 1 New York Plaza, New York, NY 10004. Phone 1-800-SPRINGER, fax (201) 348-4505, e-mail orders-ny@springer-sbm.com, or visit www.springeronline.com. Apress Media, LLC is a California LLC and the sole member (owner) is Springer Science + Business Media Finance Inc (SSBM Finance Inc). SSBM Finance Inc is a **Delaware** corporation.

For information on translations, please e-mail booktranslations@springernature.com; for reprint, paperback, or audio rights, please e-mail bookpermissions@springernature.com.

Apress titles may be purchased in bulk for academic, corporate, or promotional use. eBook versions and licenses are also available for most titles. For more information, reference our Print and eBook Bulk Sales web page at http://www.apress.com/bulk-sales.

Any source code or other supplementary material referenced by the author in this book is available to readers on GitHub via the book's product page, located at www.apress.com/9781484260371. For more detailed information, please visit http://www.apress.com/source-code.

Printed on acid-free paper

Dedicated in memory of my beloved grandfather Ram Naresh Singh, 1935–2017.

The only hero I've ever had or needed. You are still an inspiration and motivation behind every effort we put in to see a positive impact in our life and society.

Table of Contents

About the Author

Prateek Singh is an IT Infrastructure and cloud developer, an avid PowerShell blogger, and an open source community contributor. His blog `www.ridicurious.com` has been recognized as among the "Top 50 PowerShell blogs in the world" in the last three consecutive years.

Prateek has extensive experience in technical writing and has written more than 250 articles on his blog and several other websites such as *4SysOps.com*, *IPSwitch.com*, and *TechTarget.com* and also runs a YouTube channel on PowerShell Scripting and Azure. He has written few other technology books on PowerShell and Python and is writing a new one *PowerShell to C# and Back*, on C# and .Net.

When he is not in front of a computer, Prateek loves reading his humongous collection of compulsively bought books with a warm cup of coffee and really enjoys long-distance running.

About the Technical Reviewer

Nathan Haines first started using Linux in 1994, when a new BBS had a menu option for "command prompt," and it wasn't quite the DOS he was familiar with. He and a couple friends started exploring, and it's been love ever since. Today he's equally at home with the command line as he is with a graphical interface.

Nathan loves computers and video games and spends a lot of time reminiscing about old ones he's owned. He can often be found typing on an Alphasmart Neo so that he will not be tempted by those old computers or video games.

Nathan writes sci-fi and fantasy and sometimes just writes stories set on Earth that remind him of growing up. He translated the beloved novels from Egosoft's X-Universe game series into English. He has written a friendly guide to the Ubuntu operating system, *Beginning Ubuntu for Windows and Mac Users* (Apress, 2017).

A hybrid author who enjoys stiff drinks, moonlit walks on the beach, and five-star reviews on his books, he can be found on the Web at `www.nhaines.com`.

CHAPTER 1

Getting Started with WSL

Windows Subsystem for Linux (WSL) is not the first subsystem that has ever existed in the Windows operating system; instead, it is a more refined product of years of research in developing isolated subsystems for application sandboxing that are decoupled from the host operating system.

Before we deep dive into setup, configuration, and workings of Windows Subsystem for Linux, let's first look into how it all started and then quickly go through some keywords and definitions that will bring us on the same page and help us across the chapters in this book.

This chapter's WSL primer will certainly help, but feel free to skip it for now if you want to get straight into the setup and hands-on workings.

History of Windows Subsystems

Since the initial releases of Microsoft Windows NT, the operating system was designed to allow coexistence of one or more subsystems within the operating system which were independent of implementation inside the kernel. This allowed us to run Windows 32-bit applications on Windows 64-bit operating systems in the Win32 subsystem and support other subsystems like POSIX and OS/2.

These subsystems were accessible through the API they offered to the applications running on them, and when the application made a call to the API, it was translated to an appropriate Windows NT system call to facilitate the action requested. But, over time, these initial subsystems were retired, and research was led to develop and expand the capabilities of the Windows Subsystem for Linux.

Initial concepts that led to the Windows Subsystem for Linux originated from a project called "Project Astoria," a Universal Windows Platform Bridge toolkit that would have allowed developers to build Windows apps for phones by reusing their Android code or run native Android applications on Windows. This was made possible by

© Prateek Singh 2020
P. Singh, *Learn Windows Subsystem for Linux*, https://doi.org/10.1007/978-1-4842-6038-8_1

allowing Android apps to run in an emulated environment with minimal changes and access to Microsoft platform APIs. But, on February 25, 2016, Microsoft made an official announcement that "Project Astoria" would be discontinued and an argument was given that such an emulator was ultimately redundant to the native, Objective-C toolchain. Later on, insight and research from "Project Astoria" and another research project known as "Project Drawbridge" (both outlined later in the chapter) was developed into a compatibility service called Windows Subsystem for Linux version 1. Microsoft released the initial version for the Windows Subsystem for Linux, which is also known as WSL1 in the same year 2016.

WSL at a Glance

The Windows Subsystem for Linux is a new Windows operating system compatibility layer feature that allows users to run Linux command-line tools, utilities, and unmodified ELF64 binaries in Windows natively without actually running a full Linux virtual machine. The Windows Subsystem for Linux was developed as a tool for developers, but it is also seeing a great adoption rate among system administrators and in the cybersecurity space.

WSL goes far beyond just a Linux "bash" shell on Windows; in fact, it is a whole compatibility layer for running an environment that looks and behaves just like the Linux operating system. It has enabled Windows users to run common free command-line software such as "grep," "sed," and "awk" or any other ELF64 binaries in Linux distribution of choice which can be downloaded from Microsoft Store usually for free. This means now we can use Linux tools such as bash, vim, and Emacs with Linux-like user experience on Windows operating systems without using any third-party POSIX-compatible environment like Cygwin.

Microsoft has been definitely pushing the boundaries of operating system research with the initial version of WSL, that is, version 1 or wsl.exe. Now it is no longer about the operating system or taking sides as a Windows or a Linux user and basically drills down to providing the end user the best possible tools in the market to solve their problems and build applications irrespective of the underlying platform.

Advantages of WSL1

Let's suppose you are a Windows system administrator or a Windows developer and you are going through some how-to article on the Internet to set up a web server or something and all of a sudden you see a dollar sign ($) prompt for a bash shell in the instructions. Immediately this internal monologue will start:

> *Oh no! I am not used to this; I don't have this on my system. I*
> *probably have to spin up a virtual machine and run Linux on it*
> *before I can follow these instructions in the how-to article. But that*
> *is a lot of work! I'm not doing this.*

This is one of the problems that became the genesis for the Windows Subsystem for Linux. In simpler terms, it was a necessity to have a subsystem which can provide seamless ability to developers and system administrators to run Linux binaries like bash, natively on Windows in no time. That can eliminate worry, hassle, and time spent in spinning up a virtual machine and installing a Linux operating system to perform some basic tasks.

The following bullet points further emphasize gaps and areas that are filled by the Windows Subsystem for Linux:

- **Resource consumption** – Virtual machines have served us well and are not going anywhere, but there is definitely some resource overhead in terms of memory, CPU, and storage that comes with it, whereas with the Windows Subsystem for Linux, resource consumption on the underlying host operating system is minimal. To be honest, it doesn't make any sense to spin up a virtual machine just to check a few Linux commands, if we have a bash shell running inside the Windows Subsystem for Linux.

- **Access to Linux tools** – Running Linux binaries on Windows operating systems opens a whole new window of opportunities for Windows users to the Linux world by making most of the powerful Linux applications and tools available to them.

- **Cross-platform development** – Developers and system administrators both can utilize the Windows Subsystem for Linux to work on cross-platform products and tools, like .Net Core. That being said, I can easily test a project on Windows and then in the Windows Subsystem for Linux without even spinning up a Linux virtual machine.

- **Right tool for the right job** – The idea is to use the best tools irrespective of the underlying platform. That means if I am comfortable in deploying a nginx web server on Linux, then I could do that on the Windows operating system inside a subsystem that allows you to run nginx like you are running natively on a Linux machine.

- **Same user experience** – WSL offers not just integration; it provides a seamless experience for Linux developers. Most of the time, a developer won't even realize that they are not working on a Linux operating system but instead a translation layer running native Linux binaries on top of the Windows operating system.

- **Secure isolation** – Since WSL is a subsystem, the applications running on it are actually running in a secure, isolated container, which can't compromise other applications on the host operating system.

Now let us look into the architecture and some internal components of WSL that make it work so seamlessly.

Architecture and Components of WSL1

WSL is a collection of software components and drivers implemented by Microsoft that act as a translation layer between the Linux user space and underlying Windows NT kernel, to translate system calls, virtual files, and the file system. WSL is comprised of both user- and kernel-mode components, and this translation service from Linux user space to the Windows NT kernel emulates a Linux kernel, such that Linux applications don't even realize that they are not interacting with Linux kernel but with Windows NT kernel. Let's try to understand this from Figure 1-1.

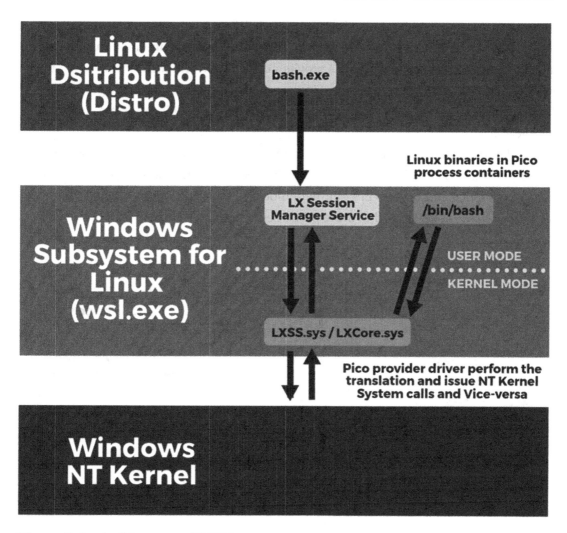

Figure 1-1. *Architecture of WSL1*

When "bash.exe" is launched from the host Windows operating system, it goes ahead and launches a Linux process: /bin/bash in a Linux instance that is holding a data structure to keep track of all processes, threads, and runtime state. A "LX Session Manager Service" handles the life cycle of such Linux instances. The role of this service is to act as a broker to the Linux subsystem driver, and this service also helps in case of installations and uninstallations in order to synchronize operations to allow only one process to perform these actions one at a time.

In 2011, a Microsoft Research team started a project called "Drawbridge," which later introduced a concept known as PICO process that was implemented in Windows. A PICO process is a process-based isolation container with a small kernel API surface that allows a subsystem to hold Linux binaries inside it. When you perform any operation on these Linux binaries, the container or the PICO processes in combination with *lxss. sys* and *lxcore.sys*, also known as PICO provider drivers, perform the translation of Linux system calls into NT APIs to emulate a Linux kernel. In simple terms, PICO providers issue equivalent system calls to the Windows NT kernel for the Linux system calls and vice versa.

As demonstrated in Figure 1-2, these PICO processes are a trimmed down version of normal host processes, with an isolated address space where user-mode binary *ntdll. dll* is not mapped and Process Environment Block (PEB) is not created as a differentiator so that the host understands that these processes are not actively managed by the host. The host still provides an underlying OS support like thread scheduling, memory management, and so on to these processes.

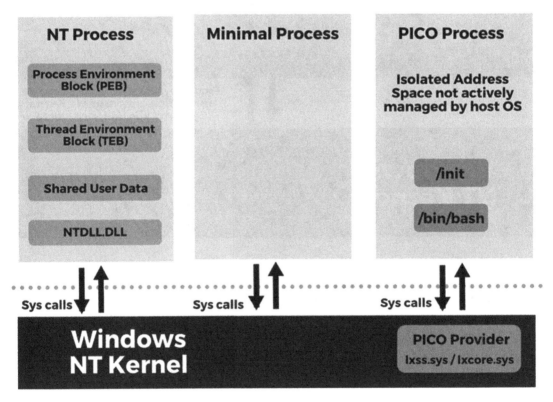

Figure 1-2. *NT process, minimal process, and PICO process*

The kernel-mode drivers do not contain any code from the Linux kernel, so when a Linux system call is made from an executable, then the Windows NT kernel forwards the request to *lxcore.sys*, which does all the heavy lifting of translating the Linux system calls to an equivalent Windows NT call. But there are some Linux system calls like *fork()* that have no equivalent call in Windows NT. So *lxcore.sys* has to copy and create a new process with correct data using the internal Windows NT kernel API to facilitate any such request from the Windows Subsystem for Linux.

Disadvantages of WSL1

Just like any software or tool, Windows Subsystem for Linux version 1 also has limitations and disadvantages, and we would be discussing some of these in the following pointers. To be fair, WSL is a continuously evolving product, and some of these limitations would be mitigated as the product will evolve over time:

- Linux is a rapidly evolving open source operating system, and there are new releases every now and then, but the translation service implemented in WSL is fully managed by Microsoft, and they have to update it as soon as a new release is out. This introduces a delay in new features of the current Linux release, until Microsoft goes ahead and implements them.

- The Windows NT and Linux kernels have very different file systems, permission models, and memory management, and even though everything works in the best case scenario in the Windows Subsystem for Linux, there are a few things which WSL cannot translate to the Windows NT kernel because that is not supported by the Windows kernel in worst cases.

- WSL v1 is not capable of running all Linux software, such as 32-bit binaries, and you may run into software that doesn't work on WSL because those require specific Linux kernel services which are not implemented by Microsoft yet. Here is the link for a list of community-backed programs that run and don't run on WSL: `https://github.com/ethanhs/WSL-Programs`. WSL2 solves a lot of these problems by running a Linux kernel on a lightweight utility virtual machine using Hyper-V.

> **Note**   The aforementioned list of supported and unsupported software is maintained by Windows Subsystem for Linux user community and independent contributors not by Microsoft.

- The Windows Subsystem for Linux supports graphical user interface (GUI) applications and full desktop experience by installing Linux desktop environments using Xfce and xRDP, but it still lacks audio support and provides poor graphical performance. These might be fixed in future releases of WSL1 if any active development continues on WSL1. More than that, Microsoft has been now putting all the wood in one arrow behind WSL2 which is targeting the same problems using a different approach, and a lot of these issues will be automatically fixed.

> **Note**   WSL2 is only supported on Windows 10, version 2004 (build 19041), and you will have to join the "Windows Insider Program" and select the "Release Preview" ring. This might be generally available by the end of May or by the time this book is released.

- Microsoft suggests that the Windows Subsystem for Linux is designed for the development of applications and enhancing the user experience of developers and not for desktop computers and production servers, which excludes a lot of use cases and applications.

- The introduction of a new executable file format into Microsoft Windows, along with a very large number of new Linux applications, provides an immense challenge for endpoint software security vendors. In 2017, Check Point, the endpoint security company, published a research where they coined the term bashware (bash + malware), which utilized and exploited underlying mechanisms of WSL to run ELF64 binaries on Windows.

Here is the research quoted earlier:

```
https://research.checkpoint.com/2017/beware-bashware-new-method-malware-
bypass-security-solutions/
```

In this study, the researchers are trying to make a point that they can run malware that attacks on Windows from the Linux subsystem, using WSL as a tool, but to be fair, Microsoft is already working to provide firewall and antivirus compatibility on WSL.

Keywords and Concepts

In this section, we'll review some key terms and important concepts that make up WSL. Table 1-1 provides some abbreviations we'll be using in the coming chapters of this book.

Table 1-1. *Important abbreviations*

Abbreviation	Expansion
NT	New Technology
Distro	Distribution Package
OS	Operating System
VM	Virtual Machine
WSL	Windows Subsystem for Linux
ELF	Executable and Linking Format
PE	Portable Executable
API	Application Programming Interface
PEB	Process Environment Block

Now we will quickly go through some essential keywords, concepts, and definitions to bootstrap your understanding of the Windows Subsystem for Linux and build some base for you before we begin learning. You may not be familiar with some of these concepts if you are not a Linux user, and coming from the Windows side, these will speed up your learning.

Distro

Distro is an abbreviation for a Linux distribution, which is just an operating system that consists of a collection of open source software packages, tools, and libraries. Linux users can basically download and install a Linux distribution of their choice from a wide variety of distros available online, and that is how they get their operating system. Linux distributions for WSL can be downloaded either from the Microsoft Store or manually, which we will cover later in this book. These distros are shipped by the partners, not by Microsoft. While there are more than 500 Linux distributions available today and most of them are also actively developed, there are some commercial distributions such as Fedora, openSUSE, and Ubuntu. Ubuntu is in fact one of the most popular desktop Linux distributions. Moreover, some Linux distributions are entirely community-driven, such as Debian, Slackware, Gentoo, and Arch Linux.

Subsystems

Since the very beginning, Windows NT has a history of allowing subsystems such as Win32 subsystem to coexist with the NT kernel. In the context of an operating system, a subsystem is a self-contained system within a larger piece of software, like an operating system.

In Windows NT, these subsystems act as an interface between the user-mode applications and the operating system kernel functions, and more than one subsystem exists, implementing a totally different API set to support applications written for many different types of operating systems. On Windows 10 operating systems, only the Win32 subsystem that can run 32-bit Windows applications exists, whereas an OS/2 subsystem and a POSIX subsystem no longer exist and have been discontinued.

Kernel

Modern operating systems are built into multiple layers, and a kernel is the central component of an operating system as demonstrated in Figure 1-3. A kernel is named so because just like a seed inside a hard shell, Linux kernel exists within the Linux operating system as a core component. The kernel primarily acts as an interface between the user applications and the hardware.

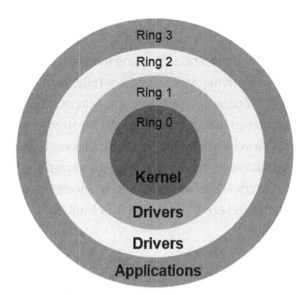

Figure 1-3. *Kernel is innermost layer/ring of an operating system*

In Figure 1-3, the outermost ring in "green" color represents the least privileged; that means applications in Ring 3 are least trusted and will require higher privileges to perform critical actions, whereas the kernel is the innermost ring in "red" color representing the most privileged or most trusted, which is Ring 0.

The main purpose of this is to facilitate hardware-software communication and perform other low-level operations like

- Process management

- Interrupt handling

- Memory management

- Device management

- I/O communication

- File system

When a computer system starts, the bootloader loads a kernel into the main memory first. It is important to have a small kernel, because it stays in the memory to perform the aforementioned essential services, and it should run in protected mode in memory so that it is not overwritten by other running programs, which can be catastrophic.

Kernel Mode

In simpler words, programs or instructions running in kernel mode have complete and unrestricted access to the underlying hardware. Generally, kernel mode is reserved for the low-level, most critical functions of the operating system, where any crashes can be catastrophic and may disrupt the entire system. All the user processes will execute in user mode until they get a system call. Any system call is executed in kernel mode where a system trap is generated and the mode bit is set to zero (0). Once the execution is complete, another system trap is generated to set the mode bit to one (1). Figure 1-4 shows the relationship between kernel mode and user mode.

User Mode

Most of the programs and code running on a computer system execute in user mode, which has no direct access to system hardware and can only access resources through system APIs. This isolation is by design and safeguarded using the protection rings, which is one of two or more hierarchical permission levels within the computer system architecture. This is so that any crashes in user mode (typically outermost protection ring) don't impact anything else on the system due to permission-level restrictions, and such crashes are always recoverable. The whole purpose is to prevent a user program from accidentally wiping out the critical operating system files by overwriting it with user data or maybe more than one process attempting to write or act upon the same files and end up failing disastrously.

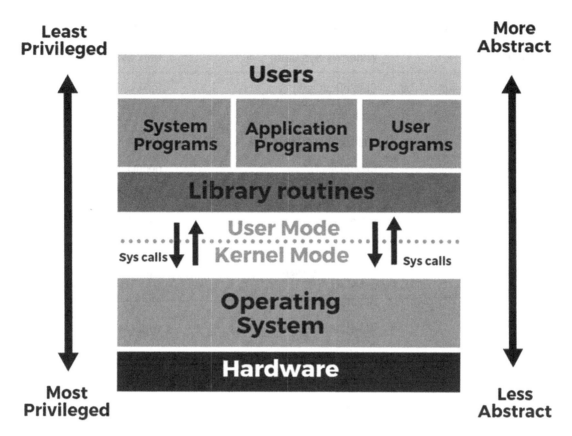

Figure 1-4. *User mode and Kernel mode*

System Calls

Simply speaking, a system call or a syscall is a service provided by the kernel that can be called from user-mode programs to interact with the underlying operating system. In terms of computing, a system call is a way in which a computer program programmatically requests a service from the kernel of the operating system it is running on through APIs (Application Program Interfaces). System calls are the entry points into the kernel system to access the resources of a system like memory, process, file access, and so on.

Table 1-2 provides some Windows and Unix system calls just to give you an understanding of the kind of services provided by system calls and what types are available.

Table 1-2. *Windows and Unix system call mapping for translation*

Category	Windows Sys Calls	Unix Sys Calls
Process Management	CreateProcess()	fork()
	ExitProcess()	exit()
	WaitForSingleObject()	wait()
File Handling	CreateFile()	open()
	ReadFile()	read()
	WriteFile()	write()
	CloseHandle()	close()
Device Manipulation	SetConsoleMode()	ioctl()
	ReadConsole()	read()
	WriteConsole()	write()
Communication	CreatePipe()	pipe()
	CreateFileMapping()	shmget()
	MapViewOfFile()	mmap()
Access and Protection	SetFileSecurity()	chmod()
	InitlializeSecurityDescriptor()	umask()
	SetSecurityDescriptorGroup()	chown()
Miscellaneous	GetCurrentProcessID()	getpid()
	SetTimer()	alarm()
	Sleep()	sleep()

Windows NT Kernel

Computer systems with Microsoft Windows operating system consist of the Windows kernel, which is also called the Windows NT kernel. The early version of Windows NT was developed into two variants, first for workstations and second of server computers. It was the successor based on MS-DOS and later on developed into Windows 10 operating system we use today.

Windows OS architecture is composed of the components and is roughly separated into user and kernel modes:

- Hardware Abstraction Layer (HAL) which is a software layer acting as an interface between the underlying hardware and the higher layers of the operating system

- Windows kernel

- Kernel-mode drivers

- Kernel Mode Executive Services that serve the following purposes:

  - Object management

  - Memory management

  - Process and thread management

  - Input/output management

  - Configuration management drivers and other supporting services that operate in the kernel mode

- User-mode drivers

- User-mode environment subsystems

Note   Most of the drivers operate in user mode for stability, but still with some exceptions like video drivers are segmented in both user and kernel mode for performance improvements, which was again changed after Windows Vista performance issue outcry. There are still no clear boundaries where to keep these drivers and is a matter of discussion and experimentation.

Linux Kernel

The Linux kernel is the core component of a Linux operating system, which acts as the interface between a system's hardware and its processes. One of the major reasons for its popularity is that it is free and open source, which has attracted contributors from every part of the world. The main difference between the Windows NT kernel and the Linux kernel is that the Windows kernel is shipped with a commercial software (operating system) while the Linux kernel is open source and available free to download.

Once the Windows Subsystem for Linux version 2 (WSL2) is generally available, Microsoft will start shipping a full Linux kernel with Windows operating system that will be fully managed by Microsoft and would update through Windows updates.

ELF

ELF stands for Executable and Linking Format, which is a common standard file format for executable files, object code, shared libraries, and core dumps. ELF is designed to be flexible, extensible, and cross-platform, which means it was designed to not limit to a specific processor, instruction set, or hardware architecture. This has allowed ELF format to be adopted by many different operating systems on many different hardware platforms.

An executable file using the ELF file format consists of an ELF header, followed by file data, which can include

- **Program header table** – That lists 0 or more memory segments; these memory segments contain information that is needed for runtime execution of the file.

- **Section header table** – That lists 0 or more sections; that contain important data for linking and relocation.

- **File data** – Data referred in the program header or section header table.

PICO Process

In traditional use cases to run applications in an isolated environment, we use virtual machines installed with specific operating systems to decouple the application from any underlying host operating system dependencies. This has worked for us and has delivered the purpose, by providing a secure isolation for applications independent of the underlying operating system, meanwhile allowing compatibility and execution continuity, which gives us an ability to even move the applications to other operating systems or computers.

Despite these advantages, virtual machines have large resource overheads in terms of disk, memory, CPU, and so on. So, Microsoft started researching on a project called Drawbridge with a purpose of developing a new way of computing, with the goal of implementing a lightweight approach to run an application in an isolated environment, with the application's OS dependencies decoupled from the underlying host OS. Project Drawbridge combines two core technologies:

1. **PICO process** – **P**rocess-based **I**solation **CO**ntainer

2. **Library OS** – The target operating system for application workloads, running independent of the underlying OS. This is where WSL distribution packages come into place to make the Windows Subsystem for Linux work.

PICO processes were coined to restrict the underlying operating system to manage the user-mode address space inside this process, which are just a smaller version of a normal host process that work with the kernel-mode driver acting as the broker between the host OS kernel and the library OS in user mode.

To stop the underlying operating system from managing these PICO processes, these were marked as a **minimal process** that tells the rest of the host to not manage these processes. Unlike traditional NT processes, when spawning a minimal process, no threads are created to run in that process, and the user-mode address space is left untouched. In simpler terms, a PICO process is a minimal process associated with a kernel-mode driver.

Summary

In the previous subsections, we learned the architectural overview and components of the Windows Subsystem for Linux and its advantages and disadvantages. We also looked into some important keywords and concepts related to Windows and Linux operating systems and some core ideas and concepts like the PICO process that will help you understand the internal workings of WSL.

In the next chapter, we are going to learn to install and set up WSL on Windows 10 operating system.

CHAPTER 2

Downloading, Installation, and Setup

The Windows Subsystem for Linux is a compatibility feature that acts as a translation layer, but is a Windows feature that has to be enabled before use. Then we need to install a Linux distribution from the Microsoft Store and finally set it up before first use. Let's get started with each of these steps one by one.

Enabling the WSL Feature

The Windows Subsystem for Linux needs to be enabled at the host operating system level, and there are two ways to achieve this: first using the graphical user interface (GUI) and second using PowerShell. Unless you enable the Windows Subsystem for Linux feature, you can't run WSL on your system and you will receive the following error as demonstrated in Figure 2-1. This image was captured on my system by installing Linux distribution without enabling the WSL feature, hence the error.

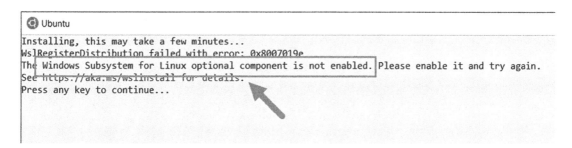

Figure 2-1. *WSL feature is not enabled*

Let's start with the first approach.

© Prateek Singh 2020
P. Singh, *Learn Windows Subsystem for Linux*, https://doi.org/10.1007/978-1-4842-6038-8_2

GUI Approach

To enable WSL from GUI, follow these steps:

1. Press Windows + R key to launch Run dialog.

2. Now type *appwiz.cpl* and hit the Enter button or click OK, like in Figure 2-2.

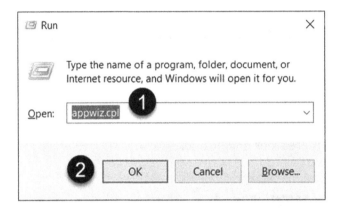

Figure 2-2. *Launch "Program and Features"*

3. This will pop up the "Program and Features" window, where you have to select "Turn Windows features on or off" from the top-left corner as highlighted in Figure 2-3.

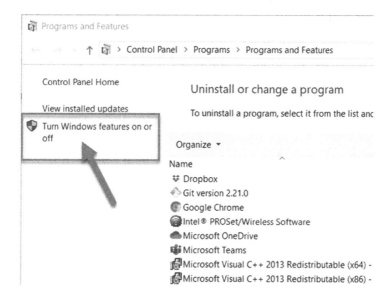

Figure 2-3. *Select "Turn Windows features on or off"*

4. A new "Windows Features" window will pop up on your screen. Please scroll down and left-click to select the check box next to "Windows Subsystem for Linux" (Figure 2-4).

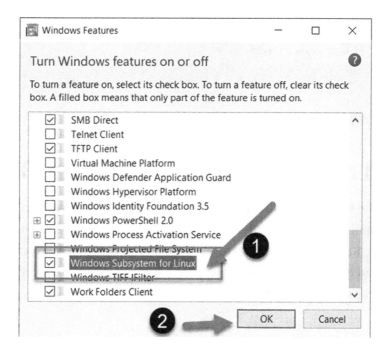

Figure 2-4. *Click the "Windows Subsystem for Linux" feature check box*

5. This will enable the Windows feature, but it will be still required
to reboot your system to see the configuration and changes to
take effect. Once the system is rebooted, you can now run WSL on
without observing any error like we saw in Figure 2-1.

Now let's look at the second approach using PowerShell.

PowerShell Approach

Enabling the Windows Subsystem for Linux using PowerShell is a simple process:

1. Running the following cmdlet is probably the easiest way:

```
Enable-WindowsOptionalFeature -Online -FeatureName
    Microsoft-Windows-Subsystem-Linux
```

2. Once you run that, it will prompt to restart your system as shown
in Figure 2-5. Press "Y" and hit Enter to enable the Windows
feature.

```
Administrator: Windows PowerShell
PS C:\>
PS C:\> Enable-WindowsOptionalFeature -Online -FeatureName Microsoft-Windows-Subsystem-Linux
Do you want to restart the computer to complete this operation now?
[Y] Yes  [N] No  [?] Help (default is "Y"): Y
```

Figure 2-5. *Press "Y" to confirm enabling the feature*

Download and Install Linux Distributions (Distros)

After enabling the Windows feature to support the Windows Subsystem for Linux, you
have to then install a Linux distribution package from one of the Microsoft partners like
Ubuntu, Debian, Kali Linux, and so on to run an instance of WSL. There are multiple
ways to download distribution packages (distros), some of which are listed as follows
with the exact steps you need to perform.

Downloading from Microsoft Store

Linux distributions can be directly downloaded from the Microsoft Store with help of the following instructions:

1. Click the Start menu, and search for "Microsoft Store". Then click it to launch the Microsoft Store.

2. In the top-right corner, there is a search box (step 1); type "Linux" and hit Enter. You will see some Linux distribution packages in the search results.

3. Just for the sake of an example, we will download Ubuntu 18.04 LTS (distro) from the Microsoft Store, by clicking it (step 2) as demonstrated in Figure 2-6.

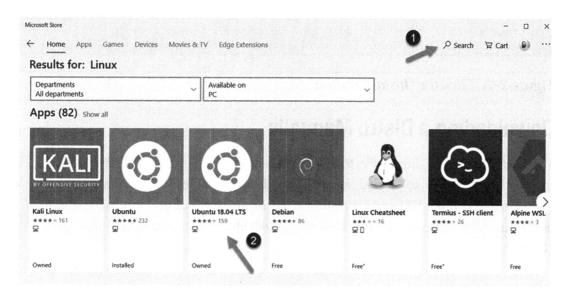

Figure 2-6. *Search the distribution and click it*

4. This will open the distribution page, where you will find an "Install" button in the top-right corner as shown in Figure 2-7, and once you click this button, it will begin installing the distribution on your system, which will be available as an application on Windows.

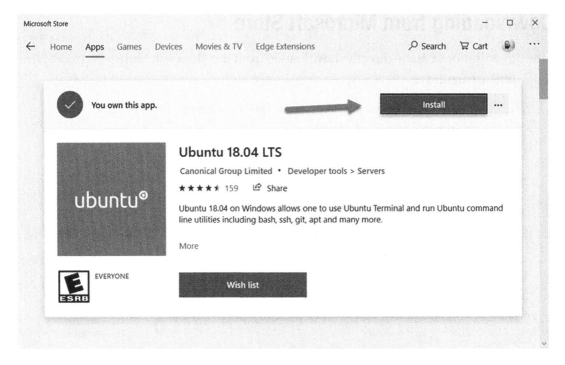

Figure 2-7. *Click the "Install" button*

Downloading a Distro Manually

Microsoft has created direct links to download a lot of popular Linux distributions through `https://aka.ms/` styled short URLs, as listed in Table 2-1. That means you can go to one of these URLs and download a Linux distribution, and this approach can be very useful if Microsoft Store has been disabled/blocked on your system through a Group Policy.

Table 2-1. *Linux distributions and direct download URLs*

Distribution Name	Download URL
Ubuntu 18.04	https://aka.ms/wsl-ubuntu-1804
Ubuntu 18.04 ARM	https://aka.ms/wsl-ubuntu-1804-arm
Ubuntu 16.04	https://aka.ms/wsl-ubuntu-1604
Debian GNU/Linux	https://aka.ms/wsl-debian-gnulinux
Kali Linux	https://aka.ms/wsl-kali-linux
OpenSUSE Leap 42	https://aka.ms/wsl-opensuse-42
SUSE Linux Enterprise 12	https://aka.ms/wsl-sles-12
Fedora Remix for WSL	https://github.com/WhitewaterFoundry/ WSLFedoraRemix/releases/

Once the download is complete, please double-click the application package (*.appx) file to install the Linux distribution as demonstrated in Figure 2-8.

Figure 2-8. *Installing the distro application package (*.appx) after download*

Downloading Using PowerShell

WSL distribution packages can be easily downloaded with PowerShell, using the Invoke-WebRequest cmdlet and passing the direct download URL as an argument to the "-URI" parameter. PowerShell code in Listing 2-1 demonstrates how to download the Ubuntu 18.04 application package. Similarly, other URLs mentioned in the previous sections can be used to download various distributions for WSL. The progress bar can be muted by changing the progress preference variable $ProgressPreference = 'SilentlyContinue'; this will download the package quicker without any progress bar pop ups on your console, and in PowerShell v5.1 and lower, this can improve the speed of downloads.

Launch a PowerShell console with administrative privileges and copy-paste the following code snippet, and then hit Enter to execute it.

Listing 2-1. Downloading Linux (Ubuntu 18.04) distribution using PowerShell

```
$URL = 'https://aka.ms/wsl-ubuntu-1804'
$Filename = "$(Split-Path $URL -Leaf).appx"
$ProgressPreference = 'SilentlyContinue'

# starts download from the URL
$Params = @{
    URI = $URL
    OutFile = $Filename
    UseBasicParsing = $true
}
Invoke-WebRequest @Params

# invoking the application package
# to start the installation
Invoke-Item $FileName
```

Running this code will download the Ubuntu 18.04 LTS application as a file: wsl-ubuntu-1804.appx. Once the download is complete, you can use *Invoke-Item* Cmdlet on the .appx file in the current working directory to run the application installation GUI, and then click next to install as shown in Figure 2-9.

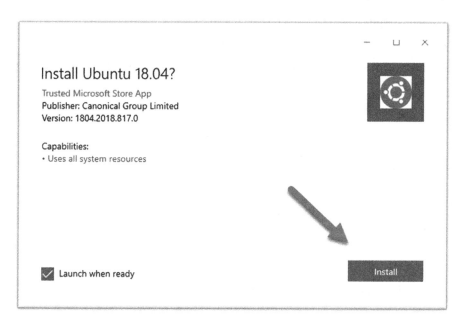

Figure 2-9. *Click next to begin distro installation*

Alternatively, all of the web URLs can be iterated and downloaded one by one using the PowerShell cmdlet `Add-AppxPackage` to add each application package (*.appx) to the user account (Listing 2-2).

Listing 2-2. Adding all Linux distribution packages to user account

```
$URLs = @(
    "https://aka.ms/wsl-ubuntu-1804",
    "https://aka.ms/wsl-ubuntu-1804-arm",
    "https://aka.ms/wsl-ubuntu-1604",
    "https://aka.ms/wsl-debian-gnulinux",
    "https://aka.ms/wsl-kali-linux",
    "https://aka.ms/wsl-opensuse-42",
    "https://aka.ms/wsl-sles-12"
)

$ProgressPreference = 'SilentlyContinue'
$ErrorActionPreference = 'Stop'
```

```
Foreach($URL in $URLs){
    $Filename = "$(Split-Path $URL -Leaf).appx"
    Write-Host "Downloading: $Filename" -Foreground Yellow -NoNewline
    try{
        $params = @{
            Uri = $URL
            Outfile = $Filename
            UseBasicParsing = $true
        }
        Invoke-WebRequest @params
        Add-AppxPackage -Path $Filename

        if($?){
            Write-Host " Done" -Foreground Green
        }
    }
    catch{
        Write-Host " Failed" -Foreground Red
    }
}
```

If the PowerShell code is executed, it will install all the Linux distributions one by one as shown in Figure 2-10, and you can also verify that by going to the Start menu and checking the recently added applications.

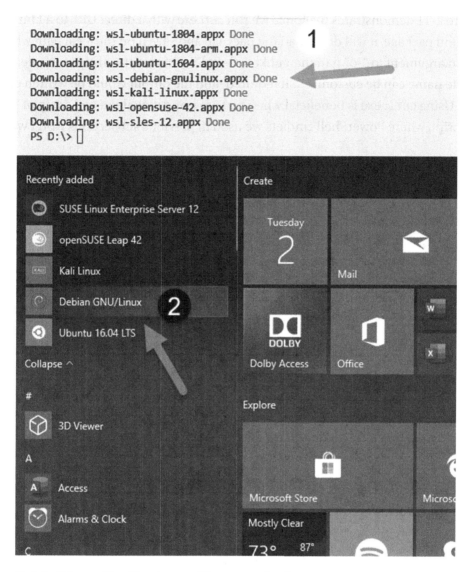

Figure 2-10. *Linux distributions will appear in the Start menu*

Downloading Using curl.exe

curl.exe pronounced "curl" is a very popular open source command-line utility that is used to perform web requests and transfer data from the command line. curl.exe can be used with a URL to download the WSL distribution package to the local machine:

```
curl.exe -L -o wsl-kali-linux.appx https://aka.ms/wsl-kali-linux
```

Figure 2-11 demonstrates that once we run *curl.exe* with a direct URL to a Linux distribution package, it will download the package and save it on the local path which is passed an argument to "-o" parameter like `wsl-kali-linux.appx` in our example; this output file name can be customized if required, and the output would be written to a new file. Using `curl.exe` is beneficial when you are using download and setup of WSL in a bash script, where PowerShell cmdlets we used in previous subsections won't work.

```
Administrator: Windows PowerShell
PS D:\>
PS D:\> curl.exe -L -o wsl-kali-linux.appx https://aka.ms/wsl-kali-linux
  % Total    % Received % Xferd  Average Speed   Time    Time     Time  Current
                                 Dload  Upload   Total   Spent    Left  Speed
   0     0    0     0    0     0      0      0 --:--:--  0:00:01 --:--:--     0
 100  172M  100  172M    0     0   217k      0  0:13:34  0:13:34 --:--:--   309k
PS D:\>
PS D:\> Get-Alias curl

CommandType     Name                                               Version    Source
-----------     ----                                               -------    ------
Alias           curl -> Invoke-WebRequest


PS D:\>
```

Figure 2-11. *Using curl to download Linux distribution packages*

Note   We are running curl.exe, not curl, because in PowerShell, curl is also an alias of the Invoke-WebRequest cmdlet, which are altogether different things.

Setting Up and Configuring WSL

In the previous section, we learned various approaches to downloading and installing the Windows Subsystem for Linux on our system. The next thing is to learn how to prepare and configure WSL for first-time use, but before that, let's look into various methods to launch a Linux distribution running in the Windows Subsystem for Linux.

Launching the Distro

A Linux distro can be launched as an installed application or by running the Linux distribution-specific executable and even using *wsl.exe*. Let's look into each of these approaches one at a time.

Using the Application

So, to begin with, go to the Start menu and type the name of the distribution like "Ubuntu" as shown in Figure 2-12.

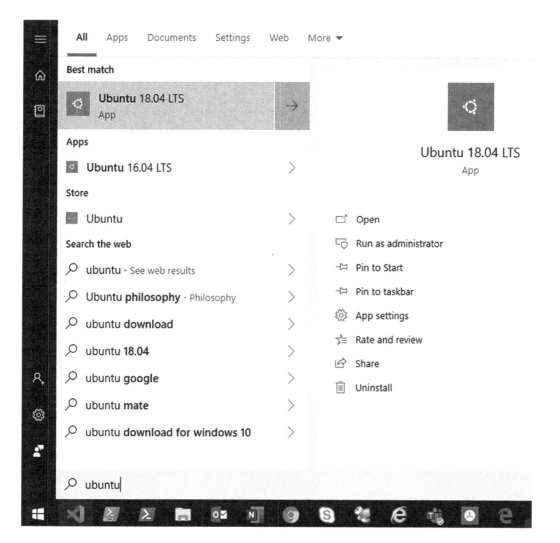

Figure 2-12. *Go to the Start menu and search for name of Linux distribution*

Now, double-click the Ubuntu application like the one highlighted in Figure 2-12 to launch the Windows Subsystem for Linux for the first time. It will prompt you to wait for a few minutes while it prepares and initializes the distro for the first use.

Using wsl.exe

WSL distributions can also be launched though wsl.exe; if you run this executable without any parameters, then it will launch the default distribution package as demonstrated in Figure 2-13.

Figure 2-13. *Launching the default Linux distribution using wsl.exe*

To list all the distribution packages installed on your system and identify the default distribution, run the wsl executable with --list or -l:

```
wsl.exe -list
wsl.exe -l
```

Often it will be required to run a specific distribution package; in such scenarios, we can utilize the --distribution or -d parameters as shown in Figure 2-14 with the wsl. exe and pass the name of distro as an argument, as demonstrated in Listing 2-3.

Listing 2-3. Running a specific Linux distribution

```
C:\>wsl.exe -l
Windows Subsystem for Linux Distributions:
Ubuntu-18.04 (Default)
openSUSE-42
SLES-12
kali-linux

C:\>wsl.exe --distribution kali-linux
C:\>wsl.exe -d sles-12
```

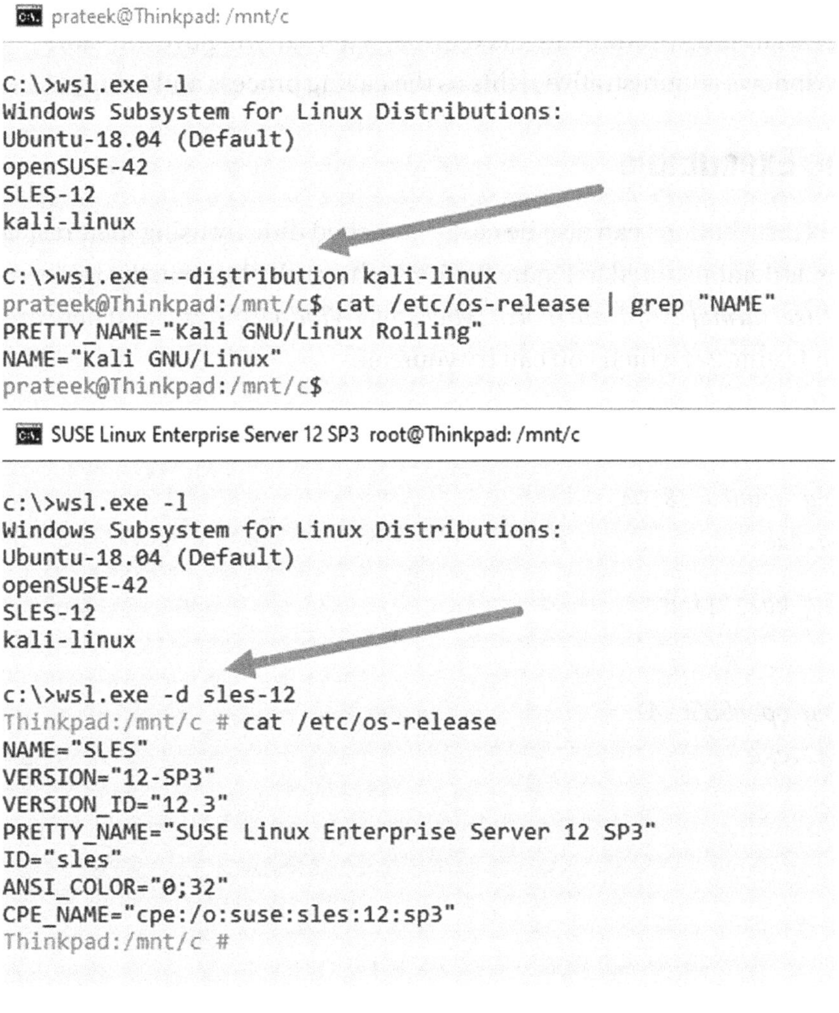

Figure 2-14. *Launching a specific Linux distribution using wsl.exe*

We will look into other capabilities and command-line arguments that `wsl.exe` accepts in detail later in this book; for now, let's just understand a few important pointers about invoking a Linux distro using `wsl.exe` like this:

1. WSL launches the distro in the current working directory of the CMD or PowerShell prompt.

2. A Linux distribution invoked through *wsl.exe* will run as the default user of that distro, but you can change that behavior using *–user* or *-u* parameter by passing the name of specific user as an argument:

   ```
   wsl.exe --distribution Ubuntu-18.04 --user prateek
   ```

3. The Linux distribution invoked through *wsl.exe* will have the same Windows administrative rights as the calling process and terminal.

Using the Executable

All the Linux distributions can also be easily launched directly using their respective executables as demonstrated in Figure 2-15, which are all placed in the folder "*C:\Users\{username}\AppData\Local\Microsoft\WindowsApps*" and here are few examples in Listing 2-4 which you can try yourself.

Listing 2-4. Running a Linux distribution through its executable

```
# launching ubuntu 18.04
ubuntu1804.exe

# launching kali linux
kali.exe

# launching openSUSE 42
openSUSE-42.exe
```

Figure 2-15. *Launching distros using executables*

In this subsection, we learned various approaches to run a Linux distribution in WSL, but when a Linux distribution is invoked for the first time, the first setup prompts the user to create a user account; let's look into it and learn how to manage user accounts in WSL.

Setting Up and Managing User Account

The creation of a user is the first step in setting up a new Linux distribution on WSL, so as soon the initialization is complete as seen in Figure 2-16, it will prompt you to create a new user account with a password. This user account is automatically configured as the default user of the distribution and added to the "*sudo*" group as a Linux administrator. The user configuration is required every time you install, reinstall, or reset a distribution.

Note   When the password is entered, it is not echoed to the console for security reasons, and this doesn't mean the system is not receiving the keystrokes.

```
prateek@Thinkpad: ~
Installing, this may take a few minutes...
Please create a default UNIX user account. The username does not need to
For more information visit: https://aka.ms/wslusers
Enter new UNIX username: prateek
Enter new UNIX password:
Retype new UNIX password:
passwd: password updated successfully
Installation successful!
To run a command as administrator (user "root"), use "sudo <command>".
See "man sudo_root" for details.

prateek@Thinkpad:~$ cat /etc/group | grep sudo
sudo:x:27:prateek
prateek@Thinkpad:~$
```

Figure 2-16. *User account setup during distro initialization*

By default, the password is not required when you launch the distro, but it will be required when you are elevating the privilege of any process using the "*sudo*" command.

To change your current user password in Linux, open your Linux distribution (e.g., Ubuntu) and enter the command passwd, and as shown in Figure 2-17, you will be prompted to enter your current password, and once you supply that, it will again ask for confirmation.

```
prateek@Thinkpad: ~
prateek@Thinkpad:~$
prateek@Thinkpad:~$ passwd
Changing password for prateek.
(current) UNIX password:
Enter new UNIX password:
Retype new UNIX password:
passwd: password updated successfully
prateek@Thinkpad:~$ _
```

Figure 2-17. *Resetting a password*

In case you've forgotten your password for any specific Linux distributions, open PowerShell or the "Command Prompt" from the Start menu and run it as the root on the target WSL distribution using the following command:

```
wsl -u root -d <name of distribution>
```

Once your WSL distribution has been run with the root user, go ahead and use the `passwd` command with the name of the user for whom you want to reset the password, like in the following example:

```
passwd prateek
```

If you don't use the root user, you won't have enough privileges to reset the password for any other user, without entering their current password which we forgot in the first place.

Permission Model

Unix users in the Windows Subsystem for Linux are non-Windows user accounts that are independent of the Windows permission model that will be required to elevate privileges in your Linux distribution. There are two separate permission models in WSL for Linux and Windows, and they are independent of each other. That means an admin Linux user will only have elevated privileges in the Linux environment and permissions in Linux will not work in Windows.

The catch is since the WSL is launched and initialized by a Windows user account, any Windows resources on which this Windows user account has access to will be also accessible from inside the Windows Subsystem for Linux.

As demonstrated in Figure 2-18, we can easily access the mount points in the Linux environment, which are nothing but Windows drives mounted on the Windows Subsystem for Linux. When the current Windows user runs "ls" command on a directory which is accessible to them and then pipes the result to the "wc -l" command to get the number of lines returned, we observe that the count is more than zero, but if the current user attempts to access any other directory where they don't have proper permissions, then zero results will be returned. This proves the preceding point that even though you are working in the Linux subsystem, the Windows permissions are applied on the Windows resources you are accessing.

But when I try to access a Windows directory I don't have permissions for, it fails with "Permission denied" error. This happens because the Windows user "*Prateek*" through which WSL is launched has access to its user profile folder *C:\Users\Prateek.THINKPAD* but has no privileges for the user profile folder of *"Administrator"*.

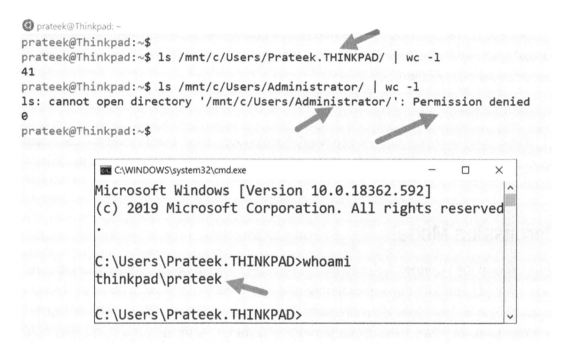

Figure 2-18. *Permission model restrictions*

Updating and Upgrading the Distro

Now we know how to install WSL and initialize it for first use, but even though you did a fresh install, it is highly likely that some of the default packages and tools that come with your Linux distribution are a little outdated and new versions of these exist. So, we need a mechanism to update them to the latest versions, because those are most stable and come bug fixes and security improvements.

Note   For the sake of simplicity to the readers, we are working under an assumption that you are using Ubuntu or Debian Linux distributions, which are two most popular distributions. If you are using any other Linux distributions, then the following commands to update/upgrade may not apply for you.

First things first, before jumping into how to do that, let's first understand the general difference between update and upgrade. An upgrade is the act of replacing the current product with a newer and more superior version of the product, whereas an update modifies your current product. In Linux terms, more specifically to Ubuntu and Debian, "update" means to refresh the list of packages installed, like bumping up the versions and so on without modifying anything else, and "upgrade" means to install any updates to the list of installed packages.

Almost all distros are lightweight minimal software packages that can be quickly downloaded and initialized; they have only the necessary tools and libraries shipped with them. It is a good idea to update and upgrade your distro using the following command in Listing 2-5; please note that this step may take a while to finish, and you will see packages getting downloaded like in Figure 2-19.

Listing 2-5. Updating and upgrading the Windows Subsystem for Linux

```
sudo apt update && sudo apt upgrade
```

```
prateek: ~
prateek:~$ sudo apt update && sudo apt upgrade
Get:1 http://security.ubuntu.com/ubuntu bionic-security InRelease [88.7 kB]
Hit:2 http://archive.ubuntu.com/ubuntu bionic InRelease
Get:3 http://archive.ubuntu.com/ubuntu bionic-updates InRelease [88.7 kB]
Get:4 http://archive.ubuntu.com/ubuntu bionic-backports InRelease [74.6 kB]
Get:5 http://archive.ubuntu.com/ubuntu bionic/universe amd64 Packages [8570 kB]
Get:6 http://security.ubuntu.com/ubuntu bionic-security/main amd64 Packages [448 kB]
Get:7 http://security.ubuntu.com/ubuntu bionic-security/main Translation-en [156 kB]
Get:8 http://security.ubuntu.com/ubuntu bionic-security/universe amd64 Packages [570 kB]
Get:9 http://security.ubuntu.com/ubuntu bionic-security/universe Translation-en [185 kB]
28% [8 Packages store 0 B] [5 Packages 1188 kB/8570 kB 14%] [9 Translation-en 55.7 kB/185 kB 30%]
```

Figure 2-19. *Update/upgrade WSL distro*

In Figure 2-19, apt stands for "Advanced Package Tool," and apt is a command-line tool which helps in handling packages on Ubuntu, Debian, and related Linux distributions. apt interacts with Ubuntu and Debian packaging systems to find and install new packages and to upgrade or remove packages. But there is a common misconception that apt update installs the new version updates of software packages on Linux, which is not the case. Instead, it updates the database called the apt package index, which keeps a list of available packages from the distro's software repositories in the '*/etc/apt/sources.list*' file.

For example, if you have Python v3.5 installed then after *apt update*, the aforementioned database will be aware that a newer version of Python exists, version 3.6, and is available. Now when you run `apt upgrade`, it will upgrade Python v3.5 to the newer version.

But the story doesn't end here, and as a developer, you will still need other tools and packages in your Linux distribution for various reasons; so now we will look into installing additional software on your Windows Subsystem for Linux in the next subsection.

Installing Additional Tools and Packages

The real purpose of having a Windows Subsystem for Linux is to enable developers to use their favorite Linux tools in Windows to enhance their overall development experience. Just like any flavor of the Linux operating system, on the Windows Subsystem for Linux, most of these Linux utilities, tools, and packages can be easily installed using a package manager like `apt` which is a collection of tools to manage packages. In the following example, we are installing `nodejs`, `git`, and `nmap` on our Linux distribution using the `apt install` command:

```
sudo apt install nodejs git nmap
```

APT is a collection of tools like `apt`, `apt-get`, and `apt-cache` which brings a little more to the table, like the ability to search for packages using the *apt-cache search* by specifying a search keyword, and it can even check the detailed information of the package like Architecture, Size, MD5 checksum, and so on using the *apt-cache show* command as demonstrated in Figure 2-20:

```
apt-cache search aws-cli
```

```
apt-cache show python3-botocore
```

```
 prateek@Thinkpad: ~
prateek@Thinkpad:~$
prateek@Thinkpad:~$ apt-cache search aws-cli
python-botocore - Low-level, data-driven core of boto 3 (Python 2)
python3-botocore - Low-level, data-driven core of boto 3 (Python 3)
prateek@Thinkpad:~$
prateek@Thinkpad:~$ apt-cache show python3-botocore
Package: python3-botocore
Architecture: all
Version: 1.8.48+repack-1
Priority: optional
Section: universe/python
Source: python-botocore
Origin: Ubuntu
Maintainer: Ubuntu Developers <ubuntu-devel-discuss@lists.ubuntu.com>
Original-Maintainer: Debian Python Modules Team <python-modules-team@lists.aliot
Bugs: https://bugs.launchpad.net/ubuntu/+filebug
Installed-Size: 26312
Depends: python3-dateutil, python3-docutils, python3-jmespath, python3:any (>= 3
Filename: pool/universe/p/python-botocore/python3-botocore_1.8.48+repack-1_all.d
Size: 1764396
MD5sum: ce61c81a93e4197be0dcfb3acfb8a502
SHA1: 64a07981551d036b59065f2312612535a7f80a73
SHA256: cd0ac5fe4636f23401a3b67331bad4697a74ecf6256d8e73dfbd4498f467c8ab
Homepage: https://github.com/boto/botocore
Description-en: Low-level, data-driven core of boto 3 (Python 3)
 A low-level interface to a growing number of Amazon Web Services.
 The botocore package is the foundation for AWS-CLI.
 .
 This package contains the module for Python 3.
Description-md5: 6bf0620f1a2dee56516d398a617b5493

prateek@Thinkpad:~$ sudo apt install python3-botocore
Reading package lists... Done
Building dependency tree
Reading state information... Done
The following package was automatically installed and is no longer required:
  libdumbnet1
Use 'sudo apt autoremove' to remove it.
The following additional packages will be installed:
```

Figure 2-20. *Search and install packages using apt*

Summary

In this chapter, we learned how to enable the Windows Subsystem for Linux on Windows 10 systems and various methods to download and install the Linux distribution. Once that was done, we launched the Windows Subsystem for Linux for first use, followed by setup, configuration, and user management. Going forward in the next chapter, we are going to learn to build mixed experience between Windows and Linux environments by bridging the gap between the two operating systems and providing the best of two worlds to developers and system administrators.

## CHAPTER 3

Building Mixed Experiences

The most powerful use case of the Windows Subsystem for Linux is the ability to build mixed experiences between Windows and Linux operating systems, which are so seamless that it feels like there is no friction at all. After all, the whole idea was to cherry-pick the best of both worlds by providing tools and configurations to bridge the gap between the two operating systems.

In this chapter, we are going to cover WSL's launch configurations to mount Windows file systems automatically, setting up entries in the host file and running Windows processes and executables from WSL. Later in this chapter, we will also cover how to translate Windows path to Linux path and vice versa and finally learn about shared environment variables.

Let's start with launch configurations of the Windows Subsystem for Linux.

WSL Launch Configuration – `wsl.conf`

WSL allows you to set launch configurations for all distribution packages independently using a file located at /etc/wsl.conf, and whenever WSL is launched, the configuration is applied automatically. This configuration file follows the INI file format, which is a standard file format for configuration files for software, with a basic structure composed of [sections], properties, and values (key=value pair) saved in a text file. This file is not created by default, and if this file doesn't exist in your WSL environment, you can also create one yourself.

© Prateek Singh 2020
P. Singh, *Learn Windows Subsystem for Linux*, https://doi.org/10.1007/978-1-4842-6038-8_3

The Windows Subsystem for Linux will detect and parse this file at launch to obtain the configuration settings, which come under the three following sections:

1. [automount]

2. [network]

3. [interop]

We will start with the [automount] section first and will look at some examples to understand this better.

[automount] Section

As the name suggests, this section controls how you mount various file systems in the Linux distribution automatically at the launch. These settings can control how and where your Windows file system fixed drives are mounted on WSL.

Table 3-1 provides a list of properties and their respective values that are allowed in this section.

Table 3-1. *List of optional properties under [automount] section*

Property	Value	Default	Description
enabled	boolean	true	When set to true, auto mounts fixed drives such as C:\ or D:\ with drvfs under directory /mnt.
mountFsTab	boolean	true	When set to true, auto mounts other file systems, like SMB shares, that are declared in the /etc/fstab file.
root	String	/mnt/	Specify the default mount location of your fixed drives; that means if we declare /test/ as value of root property, then my fixed drive would be mounted as /test/c, /test/d, and so on.
options	comma separated list	empty string	This value is appended to the default drvfs mount options string.

By default, WSL mounts your Windows file system drives in the /mnt/ folder in the Linux distribution, like /mnt/c/ for the C:\ drive and /mnt/d/ for the D:\ drive using a WSL file system plug-in known as drvfs. We will deep dive into drvfs and file systems later in the book. For now, let's suppose that we want to mount our fixed drives with drvfs on a folder other than /mnt/ folder, and then we can define that under the root property of the [automount] section as a value.

As demonstrated in Figure 3-1, once we have configured /test/ folder under the root property in the /etc/wsl.conf file as the default folder to mount Windows drives and restarted WSL, then it will automatically mount fixed drives; in my case, C:\ and D:\ drives on the /test/ folder in the Linux distribution at its next launch.

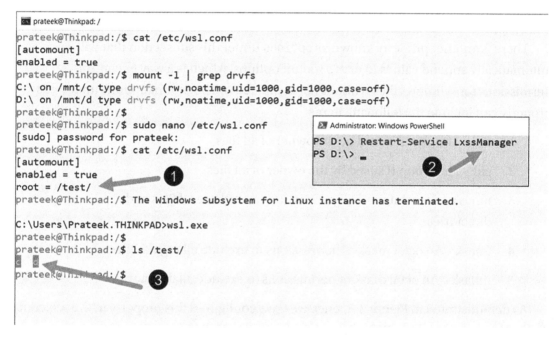

Figure 3-1. *Root folder to mount Windows drives*

Note   For the changes to take effect, you have to restart the LxssManager service on Windows or terminate and relaunch the Windows Subsystem for Linux. Unless you do that, you may not see your Windows drives mounted on your root folder.

Now, if I check the mounted drives on my WSL and only select the ones with keyword drvfs as demonstrated in Figure 3-2, then it will show drives that are getting mounted through the [automount] section of wsl.conf file. The grep command we used in our example filters/searches for a particular pattern of characters (drvfs in our case) and displays all output lines that are piped from the mount command containing that pattern.

```
prateek@Thinkpad: /
prateek@Thinkpad:/$
prateek@Thinkpad:/$ mount | grep drvfs
C:\ on /test/c type drvfs (rw,noatime,uid=1000,gid=1000,case=off)
D:\ on /test/d type drvfs (rw,noatime,uid=1000,gid=1000,case=off)
prateek@Thinkpad:/$
```

Figure 3-2. *Verifying the drives and the file system*

There is another property known as options under this subsection that will automatically append values to drvfs mount options, which is a way to control permissions for Windows files without Linux metadata. The mount options under this property can include the following items:

1. uid – The user ID used by the owner of all files

2. gid – The group ID used by the owner of all files

3. umask – An octal mask of permissions to exclude all files and directories

4. fmask – An octal mask of permissions to exclude all regular files

5. dmask – An octal mask of permissions to exclude all directories

As demonstrated in Figure 3-3, once we have configured this property in the wsl.conf file and have restarted our WSL distro, it will then append the mount options we have provided to the mounted folders.

```
prateek@Thinkpad: /
prateek@Thinkpad:/$
prateek@Thinkpad:/$ sudo nano /etc/wsl.conf
prateek@Thinkpad:/$ mount -l |grep drvfs
C:\ on /test/c type drvfs (rw,noatime,uid=1000,gid=1000,case=off)
D:\ on /test/d type drvfs (rw,noatime,uid=1000,gid=1000,case=off)
prateek@Thinkpad:/$ whoami
prateek
prateek@Thinkpad:/$ clear
prateek@Thinkpad:/$
prateek@Thinkpad:/$ cat /etc/passwd | tail -n 2
prateek:x:1000:1000:,,,:/home/prateek:/bin/bash
john:x:1001:1001:,,,:/home/john:/bin/bash
prateek@Thinkpad:/$
prateek@Thinkpad:/$ whoami
prateek
prateek@Thinkpad:/$ sudo nano /etc/wsl.conf
prateek@Thinkpad:/$ cat /etc/wsl.conf
[automount]
enabled = true
root = /test/
options = uid=1001,gid=1001
prateek@Thinkpad:/$ The Windows Subsystem for Linux instance has terminated.

C:\Users\Prateek.THINKPAD>wsl
prateek@Thinkpad:/test/c/Users/Prateek.THINKPAD$ cd /
prateek@Thinkpad:/$ mount -l | grep drvfs
C:\ on /test/c type drvfs (rw,noatime,uid=1001,gid=1001,case=off)
D:\ on /test/d type drvfs (rw,noatime,uid=1001,gid=1001,case=off)
prateek@Thinkpad:/$
```

Changed the uid and gid in wsl.conf file for a different user and relaunched WSL for changes to take effect.

Figure 3-3.   *Setting drvfs mount options through wsl.conf file*

Now let's look at the [network] section and understand how we can utilize this to set up DNS entries and host-to-IP-address mapping in a WSL environment.

[network] Section

The [network] section of the WSL configuration file provides two important properties as listed in Table 3-2, which can be used to tweak and control the domain name resolution and the way in which your host file (host-to-IP-address mapping) is configured on your Windows Subsystem for Linux.

Table 3-2. *List of optional properties under [network] section*

Property	Value	Default	Description
generateHosts	boolean	true	If set to true, WSL automatically generates /etc/hosts with host-to-IP-address mappings from the Windows hosts file: %WINDIR%\System32\drivers\etc\hosts.
generateResolvConf	boolean	true	When set to true, WSL automatically generates /etc/resolv.conf file with a list of domain name servers for name resolution in WSL.

The first property under the [network] subsection is generateHosts, and the purpose of this property is to automatically generate a hosts file: /etc/hosts on WSL with host-to-IP-address mappings, based on the Windows hosts file: %WINDIR%\System32\drivers\etc\hosts.

Figure 3-4 shows that once I have deleted the host file on WSL and restarted it and then if the generateHosts property is set to true in the /etc/wsl/conf file, it will regenerate the host file automatically according to the Windows hosts file.

```
prateek@Thinkpad: /test/c/Users/Prateek.THINKPAD
prateek@Thinkpad:/$ cat /etc/hosts
# This file is automatically generated by WSL based on the Windows hosts file:
# %WINDIR%\System32\drivers\etc\hosts. Modifications to this file will be overwritten.
127.0.0.1       localhost
127.0.1.1       Thinkpad.localdomain    Thinkpad          1
 192.168.1.3    host.docker.internal
192.168.1.3     gateway.docker.internal

# The following lines are desirable for IPv6 capable hosts
::1     ip6-localhost ip6-loopback
fe00::0 ip6-localnet
ff00::0 ip6-mcastprefix
ff02::1 ip6-allnodes                      2
ff02::2 ip6-allrouters
prateek@Thinkpad:/$
prateek@Thinkpad:/$ sudo rm /etc/hosts
[sudo] password for prateek:
prateek@Thinkpad:/$ cat /etc/hosts
cat: /etc/hosts: No such file or directory
prateek@Thinkpad:/$ cat /etc/wsl.conf
[automount]
enabled = true
root = /test/
options = uid=1001,gid=1001
                              3
[network]
generateHosts = true
prateek@Thinkpad:/$ The Windows Subsystem for Linux instance has terminated.

prateek@Thinkpad:/test/c/Users/Prateek.THINKPAD$ cat /etc/hosts
# This file is automatically generated by WSL based on the Windows hosts file:
# %WINDIR%\System32\drivers\etc\hosts. Modifications to this file will be overwritten.
127.0.0.1       localhost
127.0.1.1       Thinkpad.localdomain    Thinkpad
 192.168.1.3    host.docker.internal
192.168.1.3     gateway.docker.internal           5

# The following lines are desirable for IPv6 capable hosts
::1     ip6-localhost ip6-loopback
fe00::0 ip6-localnet
ff00::0 ip6-mcastprefix
ff02::1 ip6-allnodes
```

```
Administrator: Windows PowerShell

PS D:\> Restart-Service LxssManager
PS D:\> _              4
```

Figure 3-4. *Automatically generating /etc/hosts file from Windows host file*

The second property under this subsection is generateResolvConf, which when set to true creates a list of domain name servers that the Windows Subsystem for Linux will use. In the following example, as demonstrated in step 1 of Figure 3-5, I have disabled the generateResolvConf property by setting it to false in the wsl.conf file. Now, if I try to ping any website (step 2), it fails to resolve any hostnames to their respective IP addresses, because no name server is there to facilitate the name resolution. Let's go back and revert the setting again like in step 3 and terminate my WSL distro (step 4) for configuration changes to take effect.

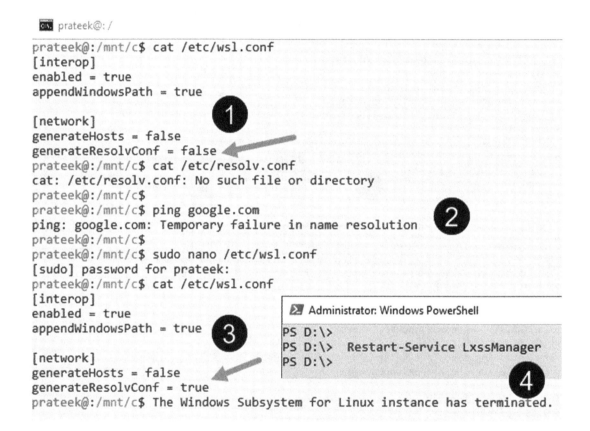

Figure 3-5. *Automatically generating domain name servers in WSL*

After making the changes, when the WSL distro is relaunched, you will observe that /etc/resolv.conf is automatically generated with name servers. Let's attempt to send ICMP requests to a website, just to check if the name resolution works or not; then you will observe that in Figure 3-6 we were able to resolve google.com and hit their target server IP address to start receiving a ping response.

```
C:\>wsl
prateek@:/mnt/c$ cd /; cat /etc/resolv.conf
# This file was automatically generated by WSL. To stop automatic generation of this file, remove tl
nameserver 192.168.43.57
nameserver fec0:0:0:ffff::1
nameserver fec0:0:0:ffff::2
prateek@:/$
prateek@:/$ ping google.com
PING google.com(bom07s16-in-x0e.1e100.net (2404:6800:4009:80b::200e)) 56 data bytes
64 bytes from bom07s16-in-x0e.1e100.net (2404:6800:4009:80b::200e): icmp_seq=1 ttl=55 time=70.2 ms
64 bytes from bom07s16-in-x0e.1e100.net (2404:6800:4009:80b::200e): icmp_seq=2 ttl=55 time=70.9 ms
64 bytes from bom07s16-in-x0e.1e100.net (2404:6800:4009:80b::200e): icmp_seq=3 ttl=55 time=68.1 ms
^C
--- google.com ping statistics ---
3 packets transmitted, 3 received, 0% packet loss, time 2003ms
rtt min/avg/max/mdev = 68.143/69.797/70.976/1.223 ms
prateek@:/$
```

Figure 3-6. *Name resolution works after "resolv.conf" file is generated*

Let's look into the third and final subsection of `wsl.conf` file known as [interop] which further defines whether a Windows process can be launched from WSL and sharing of the Windows PATH variables across both operating systems.

[interop] Section

This section of the wsl.conf file deals with two important settings for Windows-Linux interoperability, which are mentioned in the following Table 3-3.

Table 3-3. *List of optional properties under [interop] section*

Property	Value	Default	Description
enabled	boolean	true	When set to True, WSL distros will launch Windows processes like notepad.exe; otherwise, this feature is disabled.
appendWindowsPath	boolean	true	When set to True, WSL will append the Windows path to the Distribution's environment variable $PATH.

The first property under this subsection is `enabled`, as demonstrated in Figure 3-7. If the `enabled` property is set to `false`, then WSL will not support running any Windows processes, like notepad.exe, from Linux. Step 1 in the figure shows that when we attempted to run notepad.exe from bash, it can't execute the Windows format program and throws an error. To resolve this, change the value of property `enabled` to `true` and restart your distro to make Windows processes work again.

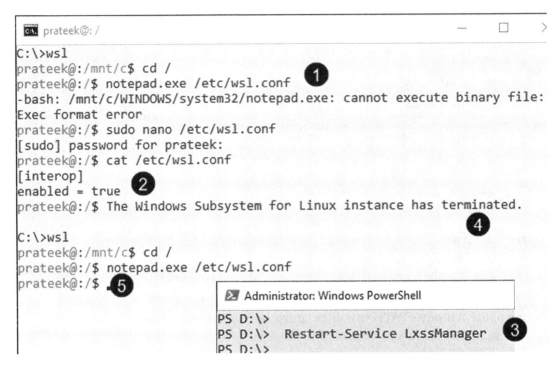

Figure 3-7. *Name resolution works after* `resolv.conf` *file is generated*

Another property under this subsection is appendWindowsPath, and as the name suggests, when this property is set to "true," this will append folders from the Windows PATH variable to the Linux $PATH environment variable as demonstrated in Figure 3-8. Likewise, when appendWindowsPath is disabled by setting it to false, then elements of the Windows PATH variable are not appended to the Linux $PATH environment variable. Please make sure to terminate and relaunch Linux distributions for these changes to take effect.

Figure 3-8. *Appending paths from the Windows PATH variable to the Linux $PATH environment variable*

This completes the three subsections of a /etc/wsl.conf file, and the whole underlying purpose of this file is to enable power users to tweak the [interop], [automount], and [network] settings, which allow them to build better mixed experiences. That helps bridging both the worlds of Windows and Linux, so that we can move things across easily and work with the best tool for a specific task irrespective of underlying platform and a lot of other capabilities which were earlier trapped into Windows and Linux ecosystems separately.

Now we'll learn to take these mixed experiences between Windows and WSL to another level through the ability to share environment variables with configurable values across operating systems that can exist on both sides and translation of file system paths from Linux to Windows and vice versa. Let's start with the path translation first.

Windows-Linux Path Translation – wslpath

wslpath is a utility that performs translation from WSL path to Windows path and vice versa. Following is the syntax to use this utility and Table 3-4 lists all the output parameters that can be used with wslpath.

Syntax:

```
wslpath [-m|-u|-w|-h] NAME[:line[:col]]
```

Table 3-4. *Lists of the output type options*

Parameter	Description
-a	Prints Windows to Unix absolute path format
-w	Prints Windows form of Unix path
-m	Prints Windows form of Unix path, but with forward slashes /
-u	Prints Unix form of Windows path; is the default parameter

To understand this tool better, Listing 3-1 and Figure 3-9 demonstrated some examples to perform path translations.

Listing 3-1. Using wslpath utility to translate the paths

```
# by default translates Windows path to WSL path, equivalent to `-u`
wslpath 'C:\Users'

# you can also use '-a' to translate Windows path to Absolute WSL path
format
wslpath -a 'temfile.txt'

# translates WSL path to Windows path using '-w'
wslpath -w '/mnt/c/Users'

# translates WSL path to Windows path using '-m'
# but with forward slash '/' instead of backward slash '\'
wslpath -m '/mnt/c/Users'
```

```
prateek@: /mnt/c
prateek@:/mnt/c$
prateek@:/mnt/c$ # by default translates Windows path to WSL path, equivalent to `-u`
prateek@:/mnt/c$ wslpath 'C:\Users'
/mnt/c/Users
prateek@:/mnt/c$
prateek@:/mnt/c$ # you can also use '-a' to translate Windows path to Absolute WSL path format
prateek@:/mnt/c$ wslpath -a 'temfile.txt'
/mnt/c/temfile.txt
prateek@:/mnt/c$
prateek@:/mnt/c$ # translates WSL path to Windows path using '-w'
prateek@:/mnt/c$ wslpath -w '/mnt/c/Users'
C:\Users
prateek@:/mnt/c$
prateek@:/mnt/c$ # translates WSL path to Windows path using '-m'
prateek@:/mnt/c$ # but with forward slash '/' instead of backward slash '\'
prateek@:/mnt/c$ wslpath -m '/mnt/c/Users'
C:/Users
prateek@:/mnt/c$ _
```

Figure 3-9. *Using wslpath utility to translate paths*

This utility can come very handy when we want to run files on Windows operating system from WSL, like in the following example in Figure 3-10, I am running a PowerShell script placed on my Windows file system, and using `wslpath`, I was able to translate it to the Unix path and launch this PowerShell script file through `pwsh` (that is the open source version of PowerShell that runs on Linux) inside the Windows Subsystem for Linux. If we look closely in the following example, we are using `wslpath` command inside a $( ); this is known as command substitution and allows the output of a command to replace the command itself, which in our example is a Linux path of PowerShell script file on Windows. Bash performs the expansion by executing the command in $(<command>) in a subshell environment and then replacing the command substitution with the output of the command.

```
prateek@Thinkpad: ~
prateek@Thinkpad:~$
prateek@Thinkpad:~$ wslpath "D:\Workspace\Script.ps1"
/test/d/Workspace/Script.ps1
prateek@Thinkpad:~$ pwsh $(wslpath "D:\Workspace\Script.ps1")
Hello World! from PowerShell
prateek@Thinkpad:~$
```

```
Script.ps1 - Notepad
File  Edit  Format  View  Help
Write-host 'Hello World! from PowerShell' -ForegroundColor Yellow
```

Figure 3-10. *Using wslpath utility to launch a Windows PowerShell script file*

Now that we understand how path translation works, let's look into how WSL enables us to share environment variables in Windows and Linux.

Shared Environment Variables – WSLENV

Since Windows Insider build 17063 and later, WSLENV is a special environment variable that allows environment variables to be shared between Windows and Linux distro when one is invoked by the other in earlier versions of Windows 10; the only Windows environment variable accessible in WSL was PATH. WSLENV is shared between the Windows and WSL environments and contains a list of shared environment variables.

Any changes made to the WSLENV variable will not be saved once the WSL session is closed. To make changes persistent, you will have to modify the appropriate config file, like `.profile`, `.bash_rc`, and so on, which will set WSLENV to the desired value every time a new WSL session starts.

The translation of environment variables between WSL and Windows can be controlled by one of the following WSLENV flags listed in Table 3-5, and these flags can be combined together as needed.

Table 3-5. *List of WSLENV flags and their descriptions*

Flag	Description
/p	Indication to translate the path from WSL to Windows and vice versa
/l	Indication that the environment variable is a list of paths
/u	Environment variables should only be created for WSL from Windows.
/w	Environment variables should only be created for Windows from WSL.

Note   You can set the value of WSLENV to whatever you'd like. Although, if you were to set a file system path directly, instead of the names of environment variables, then the path translation will not work. Hence, it is recommended to set WSLENV to the environment variable containing the path with the right translation flags.

For example, let's create a variable in WSL and then add it to WSLENV with /p flag like in Figure 3-11; now when we try to read the value of this variable from cmd.exe, it will show you the translated path now accessible on Windows as well. Please note that if you don't have administrative privileges on your Windows account, you might not see an environment variable created by WSLENV:

```
$ export MYPATH=/mnt/c/Users
$ export WSLENV=MYPATH/p
$
$ cmd.exe
Microsoft Windows [Version 10.0.17763.348]
 (c) 2018 Microsoft Corporation. All rights reserved.

C:\Users\admin> echo %MYPATH%
C:\Users
```

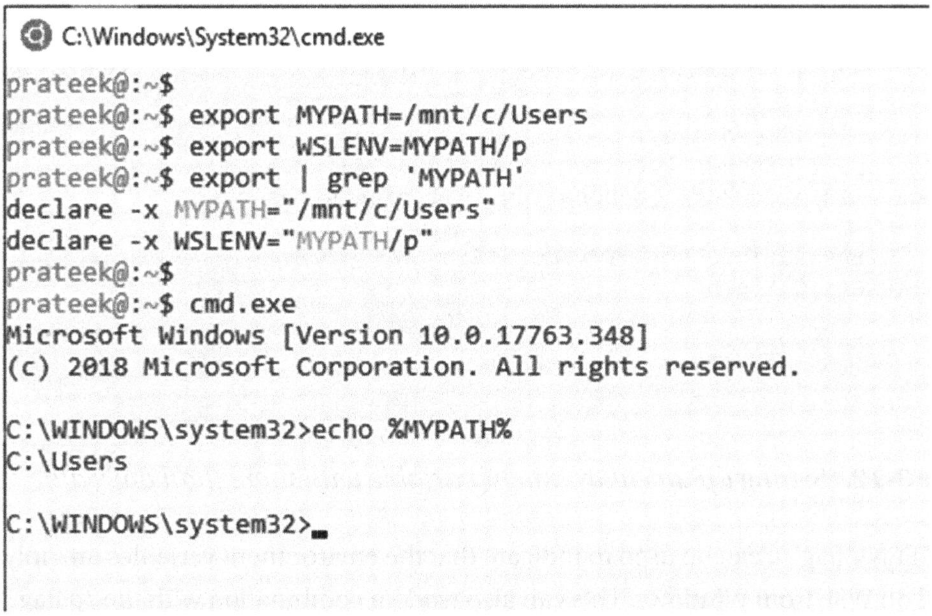

Figure 3-11. *Setting up an environment variable in Windows from WSL*

Let's take another example to show how a list of colon-separated (:) values can be assigned to WSLENV with the flag /l, which translates these paths to semicolon-separated values when the environment variable is accessed from Windows as demonstrated in Figure 3-12:

57

```
$ export MYPATHLIST=/mnt/c/Users:/mnt/c/temp
$ export WSLENV=MYPATHLIST/l
$
$ echo $MYPATHLIST
/mnt/c/Users:/mnt/c/temp
$
$ cmd.exe
Microsoft Windows [Version 10.0.17763.348]
 (c) 2018 Microsoft Corporation. All rights reserved.
C:\Users\admin>echo %MYPATHLIST%
C:\Users;C:\Temp
```

```
C:\Windows\System32\cmd.exe

prateek@:~$ export MYPATHLIST=/mnt/c/Users:/mnt/c/temp
prateek@:~$ export WSLENV=MYPATHLIST/l
prateek@:~$
prateek@:~$ echo $MYPATHLIST
/mnt/c/Users:/mnt/c/temp
prateek@:~$
prateek@:~$ cmd.exe
Microsoft Windows [Version 10.0.17763.348]
(c) 2018 Microsoft Corporation. All rights reserved.

C:\Users\admin>echo %MYPATHLIST%
C:\Users;C:\Temp

C:\Users\admin>_
```

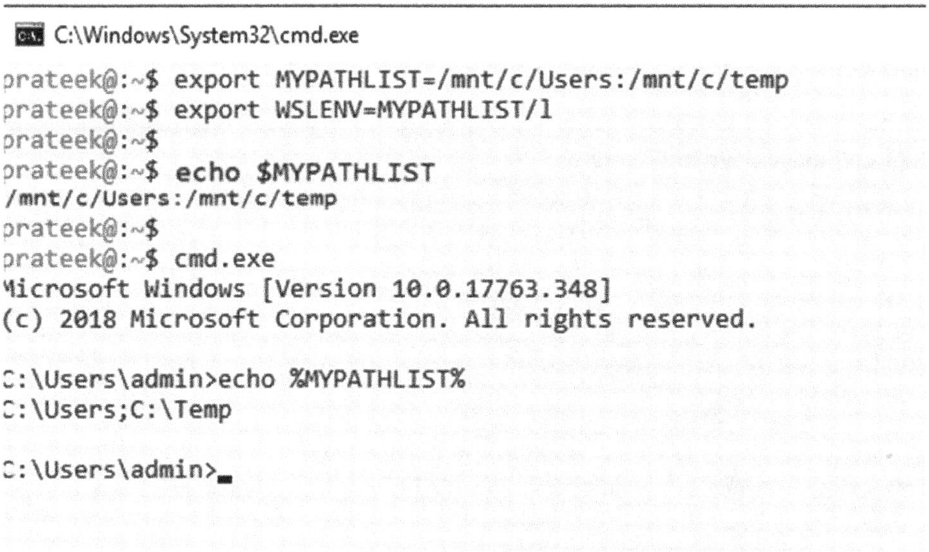

Figure 3-12. *Setting up an environment variable with more than one value*

WSLENV flag /u can be used to indicate that the environment variables are only created on WSL from Windows. This can also work in combination with the /p flag (and both can be combined as /up) to translate the path to Linux-specific format as demonstrated in Figure 3-13. On the other hand, the WSLENV flag /w works in the exact opposite way and creates an environment variable when running Windows from WSL.

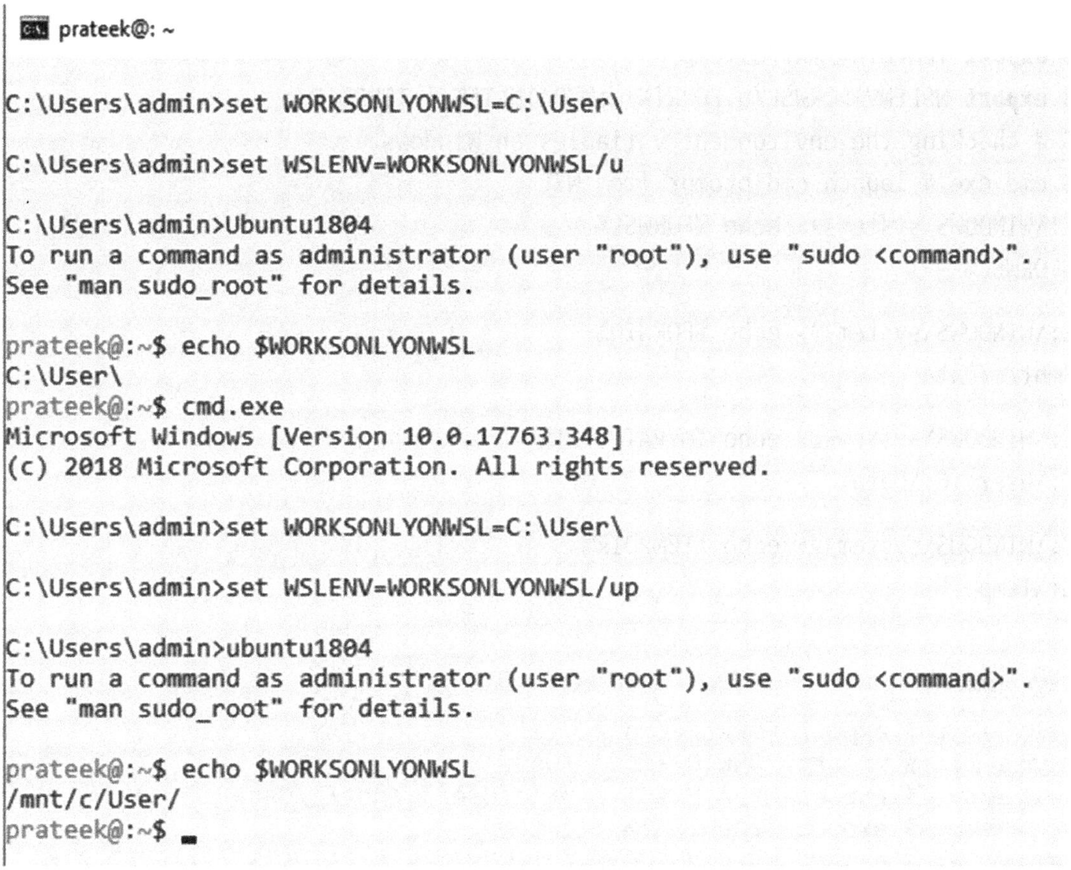

```
prateek@: ~

C:\Users\admin>set WORKSONLYONWSL=C:\User\

C:\Users\admin>set WSLENV=WORKSONLYONWSL/u

C:\Users\admin>Ubuntu1804
To run a command as administrator (user "root"), use "sudo <command>".
See "man sudo_root" for details.

prateek@:~$ echo $WORKSONLYONWSL
C:\User\
prateek@:~$ cmd.exe
Microsoft Windows [Version 10.0.17763.348]
(c) 2018 Microsoft Corporation. All rights reserved.

C:\Users\admin>set WORKSONLYONWSL=C:\User\

C:\Users\admin>set WSLENV=WORKSONLYONWSL/up

C:\Users\admin>ubuntu1804
To run a command as administrator (user "root"), use "sudo <command>".
See "man sudo_root" for details.

prateek@:~$ echo $WORKSONLYONWSL
/mnt/c/User/
prateek@:~$ ▄
```

Figure 3-13. *Setting up an environment variable from Windows for WSL*

WSLENV variable also enables us to define multiple shared environment variables with the various flag options available. Let's see how that works.

Syntax:

```
WSLENV=FORWSL/u:FORWIN/w:MYPATHLIST/l:TEMPDIR/p
```

Here, WSLENV is defined with a list of multiple environment variables followed by their respective WSLENV flags and separated by colons. This is ideal in scenarios where we want to share multiple shared environment variables in different ways. For example, we can run the following commands in WSL and see the output in Figure 3-14:

```
$ # creating environment variables and sharing with Windows using WSLENV
$ export FORWSL=/mnt/c
$ export FORWIN=/mnt/c/Data
```

```
$ export MYPATHLIST=/mnt/c/Users:/mnt/c/Data
$ export TEMPDIR=/mnt/c/temp
$ export WSLENV=FORWSL/u:FORWIN/w:MYPATHLIST/l:TEMPDIR/p
$ # checking the environment variables on Windows
$ cmd.exe # launch cmd prompt from WSL
C:\WINDOWS\system32> echo %FORWSL%
%FORWSL%

C:\WINDOWS\system32> echo %FORWIN%
/mnt/c/Data

C:\WINDOWS\system32> echo %MYPATHLIST%
C:\Users;C:\Data

C:\WINDOWS\system32> echo %TEMPDIR%
C:\Temp
```

```
prateek@: ~

prateek@:~$ export FORWSL=/mnt/c
prateek@:~$ export FORWIN=/mnt/c/Data
prateek@:~$ export MYPATHLIST=/mnt/c/Users:/mnt/c/Data
prateek@:~$ export TEMPDIR=/mnt/c/temp
prateek@:~$ export WSLENV=FORWSL/u:FORWIN/w:MYPATHLIST/l:TEMPDIR/p
prateek@:~$
prateek@:~$ cmd.exe
Microsoft Windows [Version 10.0.17763.348]
(c) 2018 Microsoft Corporation. All rights reserved.

C:\WINDOWS\system32>echo %FORWSL%
%FORWSL%

C:\WINDOWS\system32>echo %FORWIN%
/mnt/c/Data

C:\WINDOWS\system32>echo %MYPATHLIST%
C:\Users;C:\Data

C:\WINDOWS\system32>echo %TEMPDIR%
C:\Temp
```

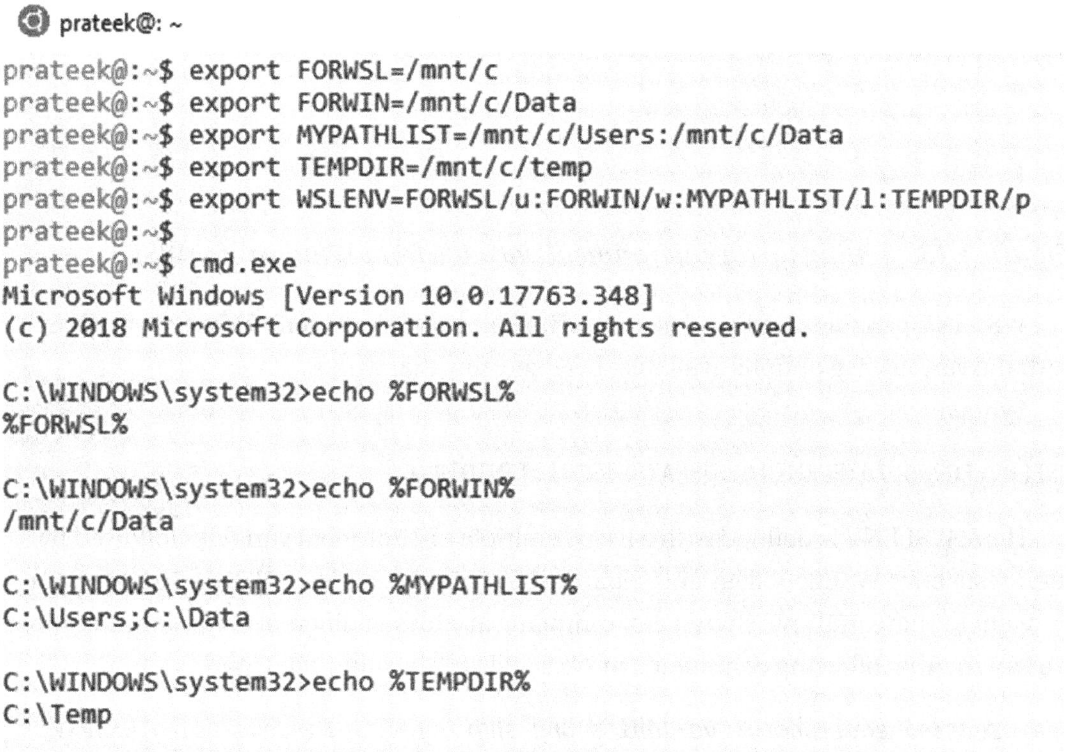

Figure 3-14. *Setting up more than one environment variable at a time*

Summary

In this chapter, we learned various WSL launch configurations using the `wsl.conf` configuration file and the three sections and optional settings allowed under this file: [automount], [network], and [interop]. A combination of these launch configurations can mount drives, set up name resolution, generate hosts files, and enable interoperability by giving you the ability to launch Windows applications from WSL. Later in this chapter, we also covered Windows-Linux path translation utility "wslpath" and sharing environment variables across Windows and Linux operating systems using WSLENV. In the next chapter, we will look at the management of Windows Subsystem for Linux distributions, like setup, backup, restore, and distro customizations.

## CHAPTER 4

Managing WSL Distributions

In this chapter, we are going to learn to manage our Linux distributions on WSL, which can be anything from setting a default distribution, backing up configurations and settings using the export feature, or restoring the distro with the import feature. More than that, we will also look into ways to unregister, uninstall, and reinstall a Linux distribution and, toward the end of this chapter, create a custom Linux distribution for WSL.

Let's start with getting a list of the Linux distributions on your system.

List Distributions

First thing first, before we can even manage our WSL distributions, we have to determine the Linux distributions installed on our machine. In order to achieve that on Windows 10 version 1903 or later, we can use wsl.exe with "-l" or "--list"; this will list all the available Linux distributions. Please note in Figure 4-1, one of the distributions is highlighted as the "default" distribution. That means this will be launched when we run wsl.exe and any command-line arguments are passed to this distribution:

```
wsl -l
wsl --list
```

© Prateek Singh 2020
P. Singh, *Learn Windows Subsystem for Linux*, https://doi.org/10.1007/978-1-4842-6038-8_4

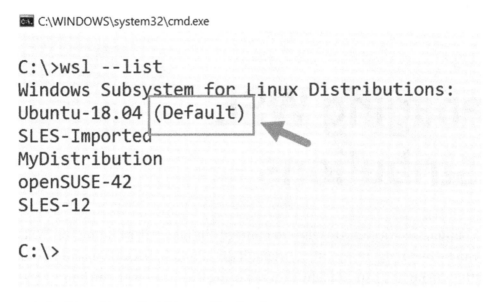

Figure 4-1. *List of installed Linux distributions*

There is another parameter --running that will only list the Linux distributions that are currently running, but you can only use this along with the --list parameter switch:

```
wsl -list --running
```

As you can see in Figure 4-2, once we launch a Linux distribution in step 2, it appears in the list of running distributions.

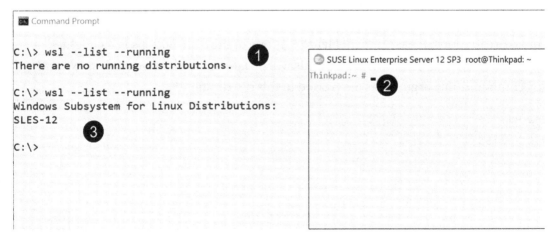

Figure 4-2. *List all the running Linux distributions*

Now that we know how to list our Linux distributions, let's figure out how to set one of these Linux distributions as the default distribution for WSL.

Set Default Distro

To set a default distribution, we use the `--setdefault` or `-s` command-line parameter of `wsl.exe`, followed by the target distribution name as an argument as demonstrated in Figure 4-3.

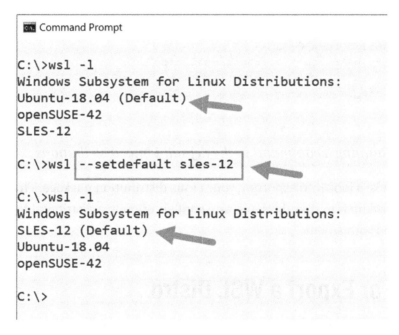

Figure 4-3. *Setting up the default Linux distributions in WSL*

That also means that any command you pass to `wsl.exe` will, by default, be executed in your default Linux distribution as demonstrated in Figure 4-4, and simply running wsl.exe will launch a session of the default Linux distribution.

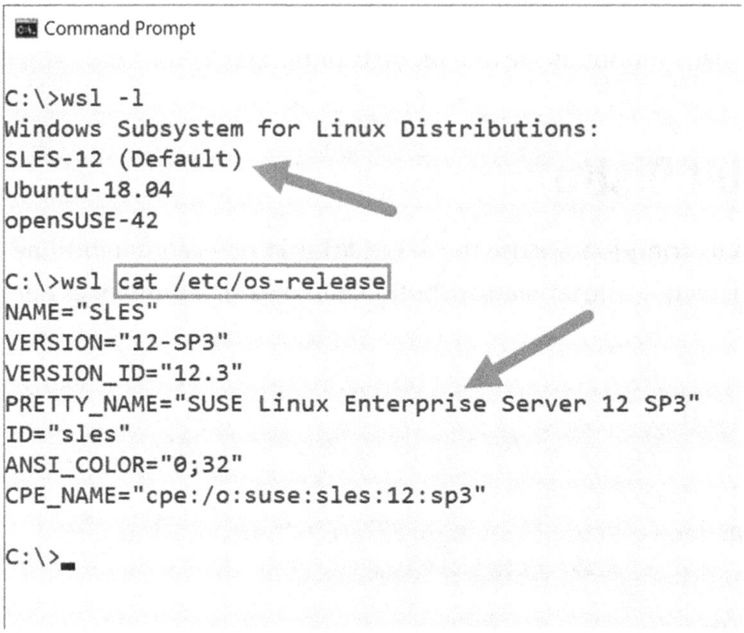

```
CMD  Command Prompt

C:\>wsl -l
Windows Subsystem for Linux Distributions:
SLES-12 (Default)
Ubuntu-18.04
openSUSE-42

C:\>wsl cat /etc/os-release
NAME="SLES"
VERSION="12-SP3"
VERSION_ID="12.3"
PRETTY_NAME="SUSE Linux Enterprise Server 12 SP3"
ID="sles"
ANSI_COLOR="0;32"
CPE_NAME="cpe:/o:suse:sles:12:sp3"

C:\>
```

Figure 4-4. *Running a command in the default Linux distributions*

Now let's take a look into exporting your Linux distribution package. The whole purpose of a backup is to save the setup and configuration in a distributable file that can be easily shared with anyone.

Back Up or Export a WSL Distro

Distribution packages running on the Windows Subsystem for Linux can be backed up by simply exporting it as a tar file, short for "Tape ARchive." These files have ".tar" file extension as a collection of multiple files in the Consolidated Unix Archive format. It's a popular method for both archiving purposes and sending multiple files over the Internet.

To export your Linux distribution, first launch a Command Prompt with administrative privileges. Then list all the existing distribution environments you have installed using "wsl.exe":

```
wsl --list -all
```

Now that you know names of the Linux distribution environments on your system, you can again use the `wsl.exe` to target and export one of these as demonstrated in Figure 4-5, by passing the distro name and path to export this file:

```
wsl --export Ubuntu-18.04 c:\temp\ubuntu1804.tar
wsl --export SLES-12 SLES.tar
```

This can take several minutes to finish depending upon the size of your Linux distribution and the software or packages installed on it. Once it is complete, you will find the root file system of your distro backed up as a ".tar" file at the location you specified while exporting.

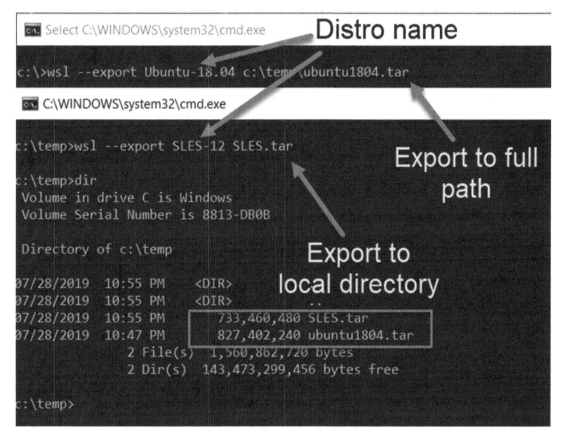

Figure 4-5. *Exporting Linux distributions*

Restore or Import WSL Distro

In the previous subsection, we exported our distribution package into an archive ".tar" file. Now this archive can be moved, shared, and then restored on a computer with the Windows Subsystem for Linux. All you have to do is launch a Windows command prompt with administrative privileges and use the `--import` parameter with `wsl.exe`. Pass a name for the distribution as an argument to import the root file system to this distribution from the ".tar" file specified:

```
wsl --import SLES-Imported c:\temp\ c:\temp\SLES.tar
```

In Figure 4-6, we have imported a backup copy of "SUSE Linux Enterprise Server (SLES)," with the custom name "SLES-Imported" into the directory location "c:\temp\".

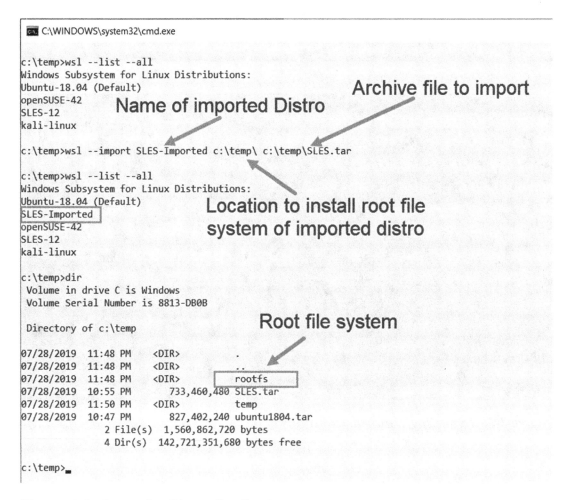

Figure 4-6. *Importing Linux distributions*

Now, you can see the imported Linux distribution in the list and a `rootfs` folder for the root file system with all the files, folders, and packages of the imported distro (Figure 4-7). This is located in the directory where it was imported.

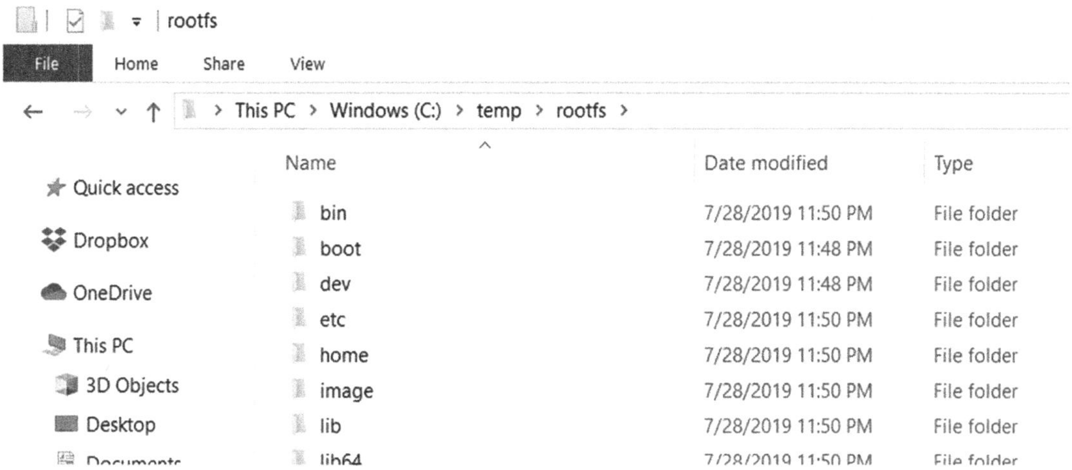

Figure 4-7. *Root file system of the imported Linux distribution*

Unregister and Uninstall WSL Distros

Unregistration of a distribution means disassociating any data, settings, and installed software in a distribution from the Windows Subsystem for Linux. When initiated, it will destroy any data permanently. But this also enables reinstallation of a clean copy of a distribution from the Microsoft Store:

```
wsl --unregister kali-linux
```

As you can see in Figure 4-8, after unregistering the "kali-linux" distribution, it doesn't appear in my WSL list.

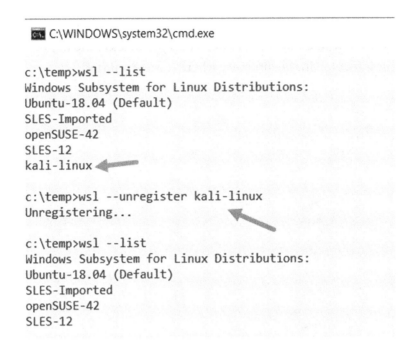

Figure 4-8. *Unregistration of Linux distribution*

Now if you go to the Microsoft Store page for Kali Linux and click "Install", it will start installing the distribution once again. That means when you run the WSL distro the next time, a clean copy of the distro will be installed (Figure 4-9), allowing you to set up the distro with a new Unix username and password again.

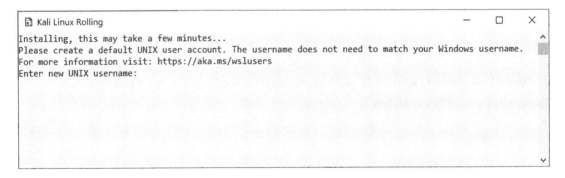

Figure 4-9. *Fresh install after unregistration of Linux distribution*

Another way to uninstall a distro on Windows 10 is to click the Start menu, search for the name of distribution, and simply click the Uninstall option as in Figure 4-10.

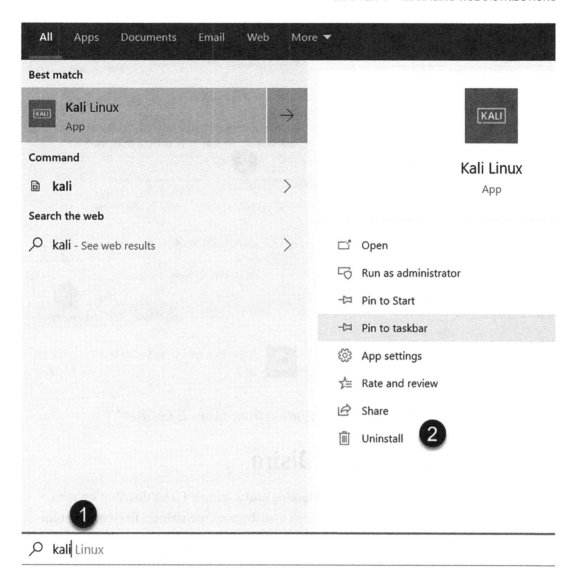

Figure 4-10. *Uninstalling Linux distribution from the Start menu*

Alternatively, as demonstrated in Figure 4-11, you can also go to the Start menu, run Settings, click Apps, search for your Linux distribution, and click the Uninstall button. There is a setting available under the "Advanced Options" section like "repair" your Linux distributions, if something goes wrong with your distribution and if you want to fix it.

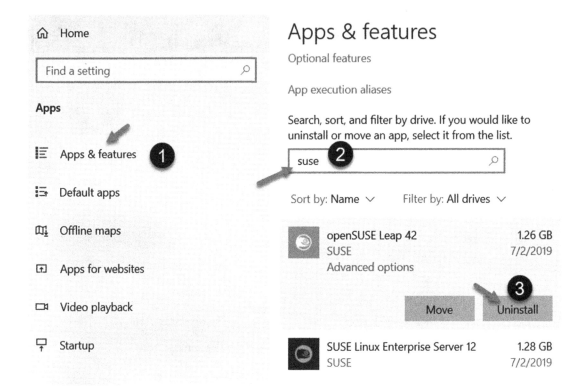

Figure 4-11. *Uninstalling Linux distribution from "Apps & features"*

Creating a Custom WSL Distro

Recently, Microsoft has open sourced the tooling and a sample Linux distribution with the purpose of enabling developers and Linux distribution maintainers to create custom distribution packages for the Windows Subsystem for Linux. This further adds to the ability of the distribution maintainers to reach and deliver the Linux distributions to a bigger audience through the Microsoft Store, where these distros can be published for download.

   This project is called WSL-DistroLauncher and has been open sourced on GitHub: `https://github.com/Microsoft/WSL-DistroLauncher`. It is a C++ implementation reference of the Linux distribution installer/launcher.exe for the Windows Subsystem for Linux. These distribution packages include the launcher application that takes care of the registration and installation of the distro in WSL. Behind the scenes, to develop a custom Windows Subsystem for Linux distro, you need a header file wslapi.h that provides a bunch of enumerations and functions to configure, register, and launch the custom distribution.

Table 4-1 lists some functions provided by the aforementioned header file, and you can read more about the functions here: `https://docs.microsoft.com/en-us/windows/win32/api/wslapi/`.

Table 4-1. *Functions in WSL API's (wslapi.h) header file*

Function	Description
WslConfigureDistribution( )	Modifies the behavior of a distribution registered with WSL
WslGetDistributionConfiguration( )	Retrieves the current configuration of a distribution registered with WSL
WslIsDistributionRegistered( )	Determines if a distribution is registered with WSL
WslLaunch( )	Launches a WSL process in the context of a particular distribution
WslLaunchInteractive( )	Launches an interactive WSL process in the context of a particular distribution
WslRegisterDistribution( )	Registers a new distribution with WSL
WslUnregisterDistribution( )	Unregisters a distribution from the WSL

Once the distro launcher is built and packaged with the required assets such as icon files, manifests, certificates, and so on, then it can be loaded on top of the Windows Subsystem for Linux as a custom Linux distribution. The output of the build will replace "launcher.exe" with a custom distribution-specific name like MyCustomDistro.exe that will launch your custom distribution, just like Ubuntu1804.exe or any other distro launcher. Using this project, you can also control the command-line arguments this distro launcher can accept and even write your own help documentation as highlighted in Figure 4-12.

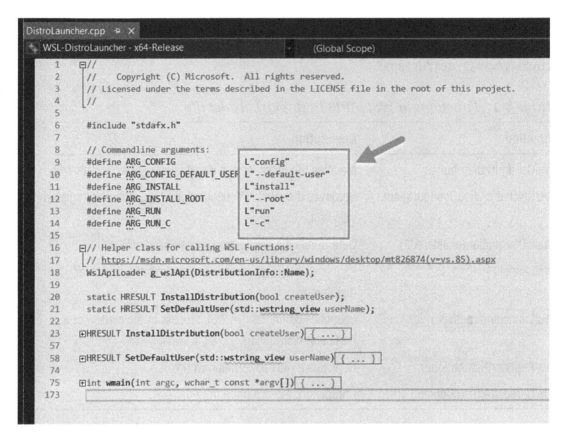

Figure 4-12. *Distro launcher command-line options*

Summary

In this chapter, we learned to manage Linux distributions of the Windows Subsystem for Linux, and we started with listing all Linux distributions and filtered them based on their running status and then looked into setting up default distribution for WSL. Later we learned to back up Linux distributions by exporting it as a file backup and then importing it on another computer to restore the Linux distribution in WSL. Finally, we covered a few approaches to unregister and uninstall Linux distros when they are not required and concluded the chapter with a tooling that helps create a custom Linux distribution for WSL.

In the next chapter, we are going to learn about Windows Subsystem for Linux version 2 (WSL2) and cover architectural changes and functional differences between the two versions.

## CHAPTER 5

Exploring WSL2

In this chapter, we are going to learn about Windows Subsystem for Linux version 2, the new features it brings to the table, and the difference between versions 1 and 2. We will also learn how to install WSL2 on our machine and enable Linux distributions to use WSL2. Finally, we will understand its architecture and functionalities. The whole idea behind this chapter is to give readers a brief overview of the architectural changes in WSL2 and then build the remaining chapters on this knowledge, which will make it easier for readers to understand the purpose behind this new version of WSL. Let's get started.

New Features in WSL2

WSL2 is the latest and greatest release of the Windows Subsystem for Linux. This new version was built, keeping in mind the two main objectives and most frequent community requests:

1. **Better file IO performance** – Increase in IO performance means faster reads and writes to a file, and the speed totally depends on how intensive a file access operation is. Tasks such as "git clone," "npm install," "apt update," or "apt upgrade" may see 2–3 times faster operation, whereas tasks like unpacking a zipped tarball file on WSL2 may see 20 times faster performance as compared to WSL1.

© Prateek Singh 2020
P. Singh, *Learn Windows Subsystem for Linux*, https://doi.org/10.1007/978-1-4842-6038-8_5

2. **Full system call support** – Any system calls generated from Linux binaries running on Windows Subsystem for Linux version 1 for performing functions like accessing files, requesting memory, spawning processes, and so on were translated to the respective Windows system calls for the underlying operating system. This was made possible through a translation layer developed by the WSL team, but it has its own challenges and it was not possible to translate every Linux system call to Windows. More than that, the WSL team at Microsoft had to implement and adapt this translation layer for any changes to the Linux kernel.

   So, Microsoft decided that WSL2 will include its own Linux kernel to fully support system call compatibility and make it easy to deliver kernel updates. This opened the window for more applications like Docker and other systems to seamlessly run inside WSL2. Additionally, Microsoft maintains a fork of Linux kernel; that means any updates to the Linux kernel don't have to wait for a longer time to come to Windows and can be rapidly updated, published, and distributed to the end user faster. All kernel improvements and security fixes are available through Windows updates.

While keeping in mind these objectives, it was also important to maintain the same user experience without changing a lot of things that WSL1 users are already used to.

WSL1 enabled users to run ELF64 Linux binaries on the Windows Subsystem for Linux, but there are changes in version 2 in terms of how the Linux binaries interact with Windows operating system and the system hardware, mainly because now with WSL2 Microsoft ships a Linux kernel to Windows with a more advanced virtualization technology. Since a full kernel is available now, WSL2 also adds ELF32 binary support or any other feature that is supported by the Linux kernel.

Before you can even start using WSL2, there are two main prerequisites to be met; first thing first, WSL2 is only available in Windows 10 build 18917 or later. Secondly, please join the "Windows Insider Program" as demonstrated in Figure 5-1, and select either the Fast or the Slow ring (which offers more stable updates) to get the preview release of the Windows build that comes with WSL2. Please ignore the second setup if you are already running Windows 10 version 2004.

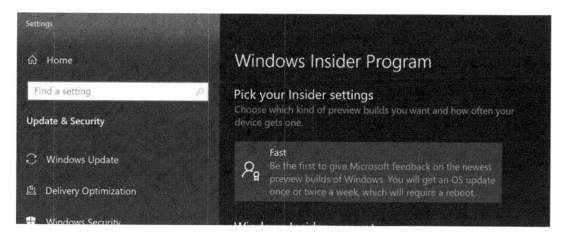

Figure 5-1. *Opt for Windows Insider Program*

WSL2 will soon (or already as you read this) be part of Windows 10 version 2004, once it is generally available. This is Microsoft's step toward improving the service model for the Linux kernel by streamlining the install experience through Windows Update instead of shipping it with an OS image. This means all your Linux kernel updates will be seamlessly delivered to your system through Windows Update, just like any software, patches, and drivers. All you have to do is click the "Check for updates" button in Windows updates settings and install this update like in Figure 5-2.

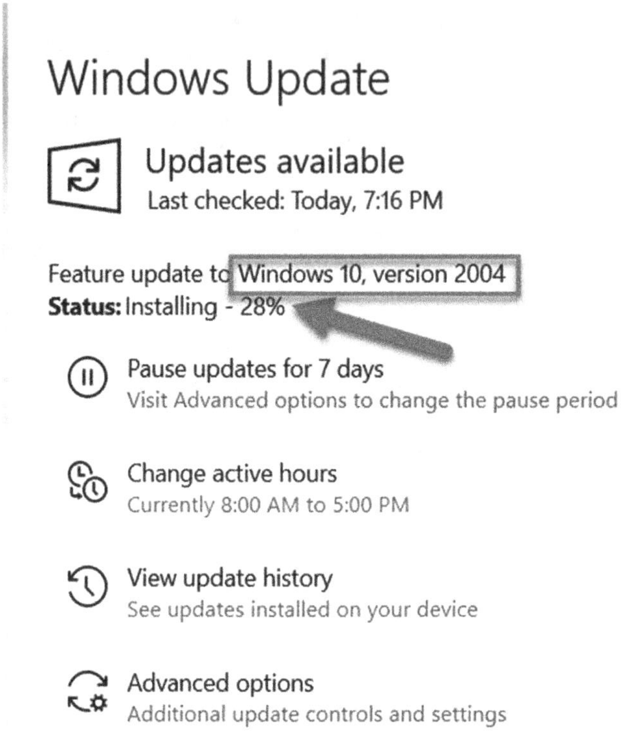

Figure 5-2. *Update to Windows 10 version 2004*

At this point in this chapter, you must be thinking: What will happen to WSL1 and the Linux distributions I've been configuring on it? Will Microsoft discontinue or deprecate WSL1? To answer that, there is nothing to worry about as Microsoft neither has any intention nor plans to deprecate WSL1 and these two versions are designed to run in parallel. That means WSL1 and WSL2 Linux environments can run side by side, and you can upgrade and downgrade any distro whenever required. Later in this chapter, we will look into how this is done.

Architecture of WSL2

The Linux kernel that is shipped with Windows Subsystem for Linux 2 runs on a lightweight utility virtual machine that was originally developed for server scenarios to run a lot of Hyper-V-based, isolated containers on a single host machine and to support faster boot times.

This is not a traditional virtual machine experience, but the latest and greatest in virtualization (Hyper-V-based) technology built to reduce resource footprints, boot times, and the amount of time spent on creating, configuring, and managing traditional virtual machines. Table 5-1 provides a few differences to make this distinction further clear.

Table 5-1. *Comparison between traditional VM and lightweight utility VM used by WSL*

Traditional VM	WSL2 Lightweight Utility VM
The guest operating system is isolated from the host operating system.	The guest operating system is very much integrated with the host operating system.
Slower boot times	Faster boot times, that is, less than 1 second
Larger memory consumption	Lower memory consumption
Create and manage these VMs.	Automatic setup and runs only when needed

Let's dig a little deeper and understand what is happening under the hood when a WSL2 Linux distribution is launched. First thing first, make sure all WSL instances are terminated:

```
wsl --shutdown
```

Then we attempt to execute a command on our default WSL2 distribution that will change to the "Running" state once the command executes. Now to verify that, launch a PowerShell console with administrative privileges and list all the running Hyper-V containers using the `hcsdiag.exe list` command, which is a diagnostic tool to check Windows containers managed by the Host Compute Service, and then this will demonstrate the lightweight VM container which was created instantly in less than a second as demonstrated in Figure 5-3.

```
Administrator: Windows PowerShell
PS C:\>
PS C:\> wsl --shutdown
PS C:\> wsl --list --verbose
  NAME              STATE          VERSION
* Ubuntu-18.04      Stopped        2
  kali-linux        Stopped        2
  openSUSE-42       Stopped        1
  SLES-12           Stopped        1
PS C:\>
PS C:\> wsl --exec cat /etc/os-release | sls "PRETTY_NAME"

PRETTY_NAME="Ubuntu 18.04.2 LTS"


PS C:\> wsl --list --verbose
  NAME              STATE          VERSION
* Ubuntu-18.04      Running        2
  kali-linux        Stopped        2
  openSUSE-42       Stopped        1
  SLES-12           Stopped        1
PS C:\>
PS C:\> hcsdiag list
14F6F3C6-A8BC-4B6B-9785-39C273EF596A
    VM,                       Created, 14F6F3C6-A8BC-4B6B-9785-39C273EF596A, VMMS

9E388E90-60CF-43FD-83D1-DCF2D2A91F7D
    VM,                       Running, 84E90843-D39E-411F-9847-947FDD5AD2A2 , WSL

C93F5FC7-7118-457C-B135-09BA4D9392BA
    VM,                       Created, C93F5FC7-7118-457C-B135-09BA4D9392BA, VMMS

PS C:\> _
```

Figure 5-3. *Host Compute Service creates a lightweight VM*

The other two containers are nothing but Hyper-V virtual machines that are already created on my host machine and are in the running state. As demonstrated in Figure 5-4, you can observe that the GUID from the hcsdag.exe list and results from the Get-VM cmdlets match.

```
Administrator: Windows PowerShell
PS C:\> hcsdiag list
14F6F3C6-A8BC-4B6B-9785-39C273EF596A
    VM,                               Created,  14F6F3C6-A8BC-4B6B-9785-39C273EF596A, VMMS

84E90843-D39E-411F-9847-947FDD5AD2A2
    VM,                               Running,  84E90843-D39E-411F-9847-947FDD5AD2A2, WSL

C93F5FC7-7118-457C-B135-09BA4D9392BA
    VM,                               Created,  C93F5FC7-7118-457C-B135-09BA4D9392BA, VMMS
PS C:\> Get-VM | Where-Object state -eq 'Running' | Select-Object Name, State, ID

Name              State Id
----              ----- --
DockerDesktopVM  Running 14f6f3c6-a8bc-4b6b-9785-39c273ef596a
Master           Running c93f5fc7-7118-457c-b135-09ba4d9392ba


PS C:\> _
```

Figure 5-4. *Other Hyper-V virtual machines*

But if we shut down all WSL2 instances again and rerun a command on my WSL2
Linux distribution, then it will launch in a new container for the lightweight utility VM
with a new GUID as seen in Figure 5-5.

```
Administrator: Windows PowerShell
PS C:\> hcsdiag list
14F6F3C6-A8BC-4B6B-9785-39C273EF596A
    VM,                               Created,  14F6F3C6-A8BC-4B6B-9785-39C273EF596A, VMMS

C93F5FC7-7118-457C-B135-09BA4D9392BA
    VM,                               Created,  C93F5FC7-7118-457C-B135-09BA4D9392BA, VMMS

PS C:\> wsl --exec cat /etc/os-release | Select-String "PRETTY_NAME"

PRETTY_NAME="Ubuntu 18.04.2 LTS"


PS C:\> hcsdiag list
14F6F3C6-A8BC-4B6B-9785-39C273EF596A
    VM,                               Created,  14F6F3C6-A8BC-4B6B-9785-39C273EF596A, VMMS

24795E45-E437-4446-BA7F-5B53CD5DB0F3
    VM,                               Running,  24795E45-E437-4446-BA7F-5B53CD5DB0F3, WSL

C93F5FC7-7118-457C-B135-09BA4D9392BA
    VM,                               Created,  C93F5FC7-7118-457C-B135-09BA4D9392BA, VMMS
PS C:\>
```

Figure 5-5. *A new lightweight VM starts every time you a run a command*

Now that we understand that the Linux kernel runs in this lightweight VM, let's take a look further into the actual architecture of WSL2 as demonstrated in Figure 5-6 and the steps involved when a Linux application is launched from the Windows operating system and how it integrates with the Linux VM to give us a seamless and best of both worlds experience.

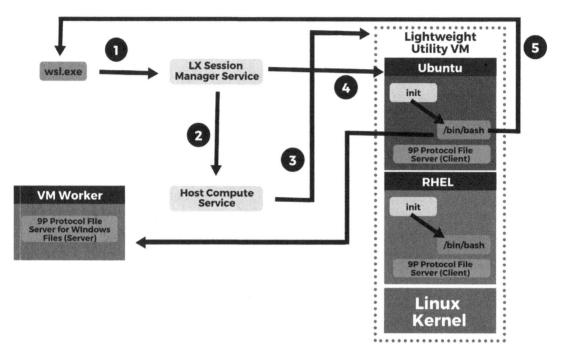

Figure 5-6. *WSL2 architecture diagram and workflow*

The following are the components that demonstrate this workflow, which you can follow along with the preceding image:

1. The "wsl.exe" is used for listing distributions and launching and interacting with the subsystem that is enabled through the LxssManager service.

2. LXSS Manager keeps lists of which distributions are installed and which are running and then calls the Host Compute Service.

3. The Host Compute Service is part of the Hyper-V virtualization technology that makes the WSL2 possible; this will launch a lightweight utility VM using the Linux kernel.

4. The VM is then mapped with your Linux distribution's file system, and an `init` process is called to initialize and run your application.

5. After this, a relay is set up from standard input from the Windows side to your application, `bash` in our case, so that communication is set up between the Linux and Windows sides, so that we can see what is happening inside our Linux application when a command is run from the Windows side.

   Basically, Windows standard input sends commands to the socket, then these commands are read from the socket in the lightweight guest operating system, and finally this socket is standard input for the Linux application such as "bash."

This virtual machine only runs while you are running your Linux applications, and if you kill your Linux application or terminate `wsl.exe,` this lightweight virtual machine will go away. If you relaunch a Linux application, this VM will start fresh and will be started again.

Please note no matter how many WSL2 Linux distributions are running on your machine, they all will be launched within a single lightweight utility VM. That means only one Linux utility VM per user will be created to facilitate running multiple distributions using WSL2. Each distribution is running in an isolated container so that shouldn't be a problem. This is achieved using the Linux Namespaces API `http://man7.org/linux/man-pages/man7/namespaces.7.html` with the goal to reduce the memory and resource footprint by making all distributions run on a single VM.

On the other hand, for accessing files in WSL2, mount points like `/mnt/c` use a 9P protocol file server to handle such requests. The Linux kernel acts as the 9P protocol client running on the lightweight virtual machine, that is, on the guest operating system, which then makes a request to a 9P server running on the host operating system (Windows 10) to access the Linux files from Windows.

Installation and Setup

The Windows Subsystem for Linux comes as a feature in Windows 10, but there are certain steps involved to enable that feature for WSL1 which we have already discussed in a previous chapter; apart from that, the requirement to enable the "Virtual Machine Platform" feature was also discussed. Once these two prerequisites are met, only then can we proceed with converting our WSL1 Linux distributions to WSL2 or choosing WSL2 as the default for all future installed Linux distributions.

Let's do this one step at a time.

Enable Windows Subsystem for Linux 1

If you have not been using Linux on Windows 10, this is the right time. You can start by first enabling the Windows Subsystem for Linux from Windows Features, as mentioned in the following steps:

1. On the Windows taskbar, at the bottom left of your screen, click the "Start" button.

2. Now search for "Turn Windows Features" in the search box and then click the result at the top as shown in Figure 5-7.

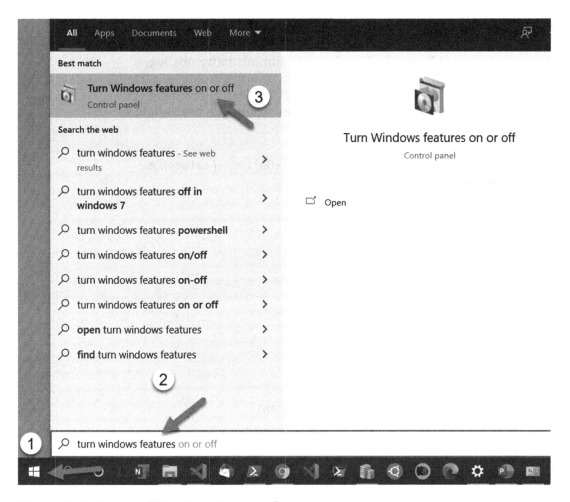

Figure 5-7. *Search "Windows Features"*

3. This will open a "Windows Features" dialog box. Scroll to the bottom and make sure that the "Windows Subsystem for Linux" feature box is checked. Click OK and exit this dialog box.

4. Save any open work, as you may be prompted to restart your system. Follow any necessary prompts to close running applications.

Once WSL1 is enabled and your system has restarted, we now need to enable the "Virtual Machine Platform." To do that, perform the following steps. Please note these steps can only be performed if your computer supports hardware virtualization and it is enabled in the BIOS or UEFI.

Enable "Virtual Machine Platform"

1. Launch a PowerShell session with administrative privileges.

2. Run the following command in PowerShell, and if you see the results shown in Figure 5-8, then the feature has been enabled successfully.

   ```
   Enable-WindowsOptionalFeature -Online -FeatureName
   VirtualMachinePlatform
   ```

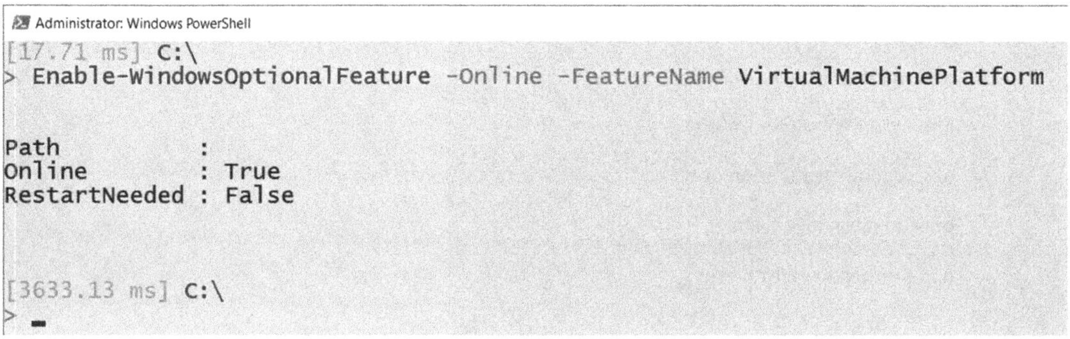

Figure 5-8. *Enable Virtual Machine Platform*

3. Restart your system, if prompted.

After completing these steps, we can now convert our Linux distributions to Windows Subsystem for Linux 2 or choose WSL2 as the default architecture to run these distros.

Enable Windows Subsystem for Linux 2

Before we can enable WSL2, there are some temporary steps we need to follow, wherein we need to install a Linux kernel update manually. In the near future, when WSL updates begin to be delivered through Windows Update, these manual steps won't be required:

1. Download the WSL2 Linux kernel update from the following URL: https://wslstorestorage.blob.core.windows.net/wslblob/ wsl_update_x64.msi

2. Once the download is complete, double-click the "wsl_update_x64. msi" file at your download location to run and apply this update.

3. Once the update has been applied, go to the Start menu and launch PowerShell.exe with administrative privileges.

4. Now run the following command as demonstrated in Figure 5-9 to make WSL2 the default architecture for all new Linux distributions you will install on your system going forward. This will not change any existing Linux distribution running on WSL1, and both can coexist together.

```
wsl --set-default-version 2
```

```
Administrator: Windows PowerShell
PS C:\>
PS C:\> wsl --set-default-version 2
For information on key differences with WSL 2 please visit https://aka.ms/wsl2
PS C:\>
```

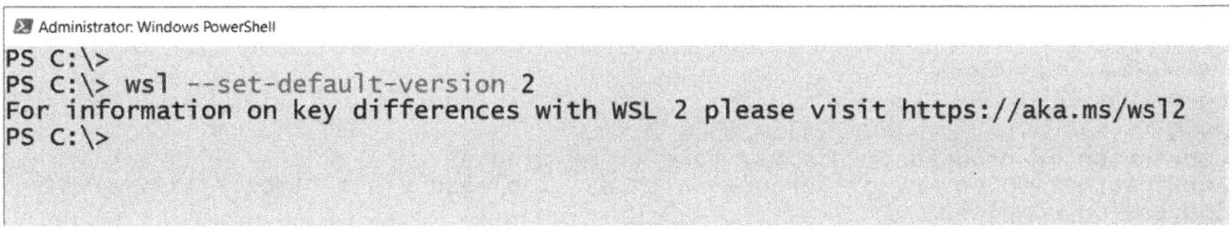

Figure 5-9. *Setting WSL2 as default architecture for new Linux distros*

5. To configure any existing Linux distributions to use the WSL2 architecture, you can achieve that by running `wsl --set-version` and the Linux distribution name, followed by "2", as demonstrated in the Figure 5-10:

```
wsl --set-version kali-linux 2
```

```
Administrator: Windows PowerShell
PS C:\>
PS C:\> wsl --set-version kali-linux 2
Conversion in progress, this may take a few minutes...
For information on key differences with WSL 2 please visit https://aka.ms/wsl2
Conversion complete.
PS C:\>
PS C:\>
```

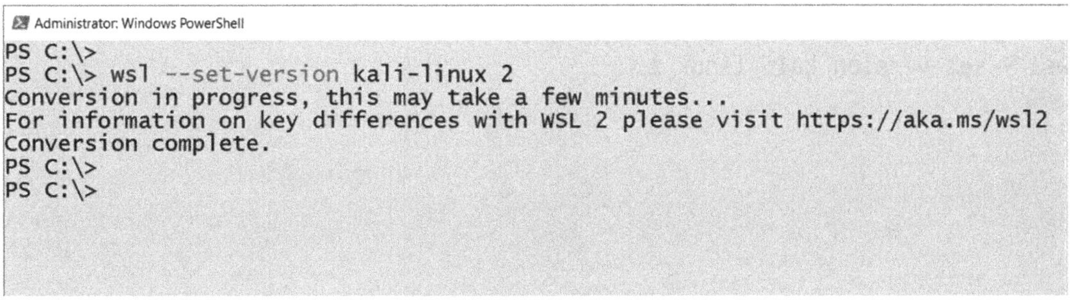

Figure 5-10. *Converting a WSL1 Linux distro to WSL2*

Verifying the Linux Distribution Subsystem Platform and Rolling Back to WSL1

It is very easy to verify the architecture that your Linux distributions are using with the following command:

```
wsl --list --verbose
```

This will list all the Linux distributions with their version information, and as we can see in Figure 5-11, our conversion of the kali-linux distro from the previous step is reflected here.

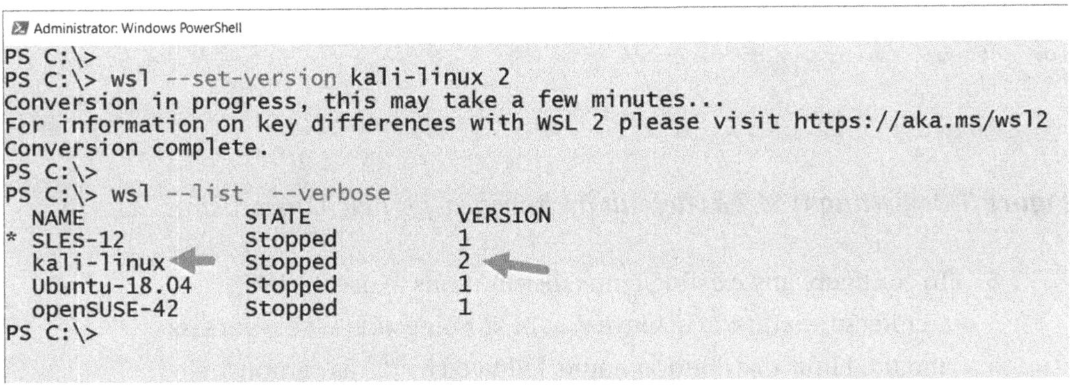

Figure 5-11. *Verifying Linux distribution WSL versions*

If we want to use the old WSL1 architecture, we can very easily convert our distribution to use WSL1 as shown in Figure 5-12 and the following example:

```
wsl --set-version kali-linux 1
```

```
Administrator: Windows PowerShell

PS C:\>
PS C:\> wsl --list --verbose
  NAME                STATE           VERSION
* SLES-12             Running         1
  kali-linux          Stopped         2
  Ubuntu-18.04        Stopped         1
  openSUSE-42         Stopped         1
PS C:\>
PS C:\> wsl --set-version kali-linux 1
Conversion in progress, this may take a few minutes...
Conversion complete.
PS C:\> _
```

Figure 5-12. *Rolling back Linux distribution platform to WSL1*

If you feel that WSL2 is still experimental software, you may not want to run this on your primary computer system and instead evaluate this software on a virtual machine. But before you can use WSL on a virtual machine, there are few things which you may want to understand and few configurations which are required.

Running WSL2 in a Virtual Machine

You can run the Windows Subsystem for Linux on Hyper-V-based virtual machines as well. All you must do is make sure that the virtual machine has nested virtualization enabled on it as shown in Figure 5-13.

We can use PowerShell to enable that setting. To do so, run the following command from a PowerShell console with administrative privileges. Just make sure to provide the name of the target virtual machine. This setting can only be applied if the machine is in a stopped state, as you cannot change the processor configuration while it is running.

```
Get-VM 'Name' | Set-VMProcessor -ExposeVirtualizationExtensions $true
```

```
Administrator: Windows PowerShell                                          –    □    ×
PS C:\>
PS C:\> Get-VM 'DockerDesktopVM'

Name              State    CPUUsage(%) MemoryAssigned(M) Uptime            Status              Version
----              -----    ----------- ----------------- ------            ------              -------
DockerDesktopVM Running  0           2048              12:03:13.4940000  Operating normally  9.0


PS C:\> Get-VM 'DockerDesktopVM' | Stop-VM
PS C:\> Get-VM 'DockerDesktopVM' | Set-VMProcessor -ExposeVirtualizationExtensions $true -Verbose
VERBOSE: Set-VMProcessor will configure the processor settings of the virtual machine "DockerDesktopVM".
PS C:\> _
```

Figure 5-13. *Enable WSL on Hyper-V virtual machines*

Some of the major third-party virtualization applications cannot work when Hyper-V is in use on your system. This means you may not be able to run WSL alongside VMware and VirtualBox. However, these major virtualization technology providers have recently released versions of their software that supports WSL2 and Hyper-V. Here are the links to their release pages for your reference:

- www.virtualbox.org/wiki/Changelog-6.0

- https://blogs.vmware.com/workstation/2020/01/vmware-workstation-tech-preview-20h1.html

What User Experience Changed from WSL1 to WSL2?

Microsoft has tried their best to keep the user experience consistent across the two architectures, but despite that, WSL2 users will observe three major changes in the overall user experience when switching from WSL1 to WSL2.

Faster File Performance

Experience faster file performance, but in order to get this, it is recommended to keep all your files under the Linux distribution's root file system, because now we have a full Linux kernel on Windows Subsystem for Linux 2 that can easily process these file-intensive operations, and compared to WSL1, it is several times faster.

To benchmark the performance, we would test a software installation using a package manager and test web sockets using a curl request on both WSL1 and WSL2:

```
time sudo apt install ruby -y
time curl google.com
```

Figure 5-14 demonstrates the installation of "ruby" to about 30 seconds to complete on WSL1 and a web request to google.com returned results in 5 seconds. Now let's try the same test on WSL2, but please make sure you're running this on the same Linux distribution. This test is on the Ubuntu 18.04 LTS Linux distribution, so I must change the WSL architecture version from WSL1 to WSL2 and remove the installed "ruby" software from the distribution to perform a fresh test.

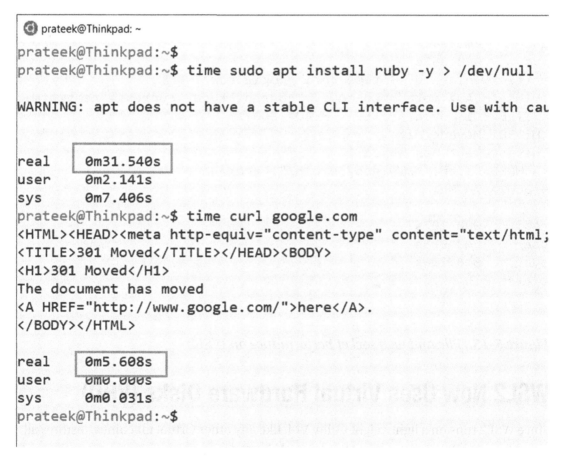

Figure 5-14. *File and web socket performance on WSL1*

Our tests on WSL2 demonstrate that the installation was completed in less than 5 seconds (6 times faster than WSL1) and web request took 1/10th of a second (50 times faster than WSL2) to complete the request and get the results as highlighted in Figure 5-15. This is a significant performance increase compared to Windows Subsystem for Linux version 1 architecture.

```
prateek@Thinkpad: ~
prateek@Thinkpad:~$
prateek@Thinkpad:~$ time sudo apt install ruby -y > /dev/null

WARNING: apt does not have a stable CLI interface. Use with cau

real    0m4.887s
user    0m1.942s
sys     0m0.353s
prateek@Thinkpad:~$ time curl google.com
<HTML><HEAD><meta http-equiv="content-type" content="text/html;
<TITLE>301 Moved</TITLE></HEAD><BODY>
<H1>301 Moved</H1>
The document has moved
<A HREF="http://www.google.com/">here</A>.
</BODY></HTML>

real    0m0.107s
user    0m0.008s
sys     0m0.000s
prateek@Thinkpad:~$ _
```

Figure 5-15. *File and web socket performance on WSL2*

WSL2 Now Uses Virtual Hardware Disks (VHD)

Since WSL2 runs on a lightweight utility VM, like any other virtual machines, it stores all your Linux files inside of a virtual hardware disk (VHD) which uses the ext4 file system. The VHD is initially set to a maximum size of 256GB, and depending upon your usage, this VHD automatically grows and shrinks to fulfill your storage requirements until it hits this maximum limit. Once the limit is reached, you start getting "out of disk space" errors. In order to fix these errors, you have to expand the VHD size by performing the following steps:

1. Kill all running WSL instances using the following command:

    ```
    wsl --shutdown
    ```

2. Use PowerShell to find your Linux distribution's installation package name PackageFamilyName and the full path to its ext4. vhdx file:

    ```
    $pkgFamilyName = (Get-AppxPackage -Name "*ubuntu*").
    PackageFamilyName
    $Path = "$env:LOCALAPPDATA\Packages\$pkgFamilyName\LocalState\*.
    vhdx"
    $vhd = Get-ChildItem $Path
    ```

    Finally, we use the Resize-VHD cmdlet from the Hyper-V module to expand this virtual hardware disk to the size we want as shown in Figure 5-16:

    ```
    Resize-VHD -Path $VHD.FullName -SizeBytes <size>
    ```

```
Windows PowerShell
PS C:\> $pkgFamilyName = (Get-AppxPackage -Name "*ubuntu*").PackageFamilyName
PS C:\> $Path = "$env:LOCALAPPDATA\Packages\$pkgFamilyName\LocalState\*.vhdx"
PS C:\> $vhd = Get-ChildItem $Path
PS C:\> Resize-VHD -Path $VHD.FullName -SizeBytes 300GB
PS C:\>
```

Figure 5-16. *Resizing WSL2 virtual hardware disks*

3. Once the resize is complete and you don't get any errors, as in the preceding image, then relaunch your WSL2 Linux distribution.

4. Now we have to expand the file system's size from within WSL and make it aware of changes we performed in the previous step. For that, we have to run the following command in your WSL distribution to make sure the file system is mounted:

    ```
    sudo mount -t devtmpfs none /dev
    ```

Once that is done, then we have to find the root file system in use by filtering out file system of type ext4 using the following command, which will highlight the mount point we want to target as demonstrated in Figure 5-17:

```
mount | grep ext4
```

5. Please copy the name of this entry such as /dev/sdb from the following example and run the following command:

```
sudo resize2fs /dev/sd**
```

Make sure to replace the asterisk (*) in the preceding command with the correct characters in your command, and if this runs successfully without errors, then the VHD expansion is complete. It may be required to install resize2fs if it has not been installed with on the Linux distribution.

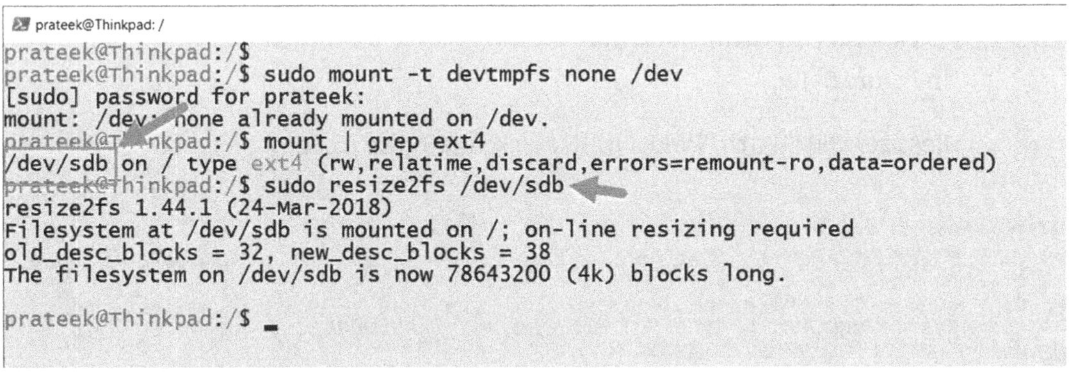

Figure 5-17. Expanding VHD within WSL2

Networking Changes and Considerations

When using a WSL1 Linux distribution, all the Linux calls are getting translated to Windows system calls, and if your system is using the LAN, then any application running on WSL will use the LAN directly as well. But this behavior changes in WSL2, as WSL2 runs on a lightweight utility VM and has a virtualized Ethernet adapter with its own IP address allotted to it as demonstrated in Figure 5-18.

```
Windows PowerShell
PS C:\>
PS C:\> Get-NetAdapter *WSL* | Format-List


Name                         : vEthernet (WSL)
InterfaceDescription         : Hyper-V Virtual Ethernet Adapter #2
InterfaceIndex               : 61
MacAddress                   : 00-15-5D-E0-A6-19
MediaType                    : 802.3
PhysicalMediaType            : Unspecified
InterfaceOperationalStatus   : Up
AdminStatus                  : Up
LinkSpeed(Gbps)              : 10
MediaConnectionState         : Connected
ConnectorPresent             : False
DriverInformation            : Driver Date 2006-06-21 Version 10.0.19041.1


PS C:\> Get-NetAdapter *WSL* | Get-NetIPAddress | ForEach-Object IPAddress
fe80::c03f:f6b1:5a4c:621a%61
172.21.144.1
PS C:\> _
```

Figure 5-18. *WSL2 has a dedicated virtual Ethernet adapter*

In addition to that, since WSL2 is still a new product and work in progress, you will observe that in early releases of WSL2 you will have to access the Windows operating system from Linux using the IP address of your host machine, but this experience will be much smoother with later releases.

Accessing Windows Applications from Linux

For example, my computer is on Windows 10 version 2004 (OS build 19041.172), and I have a simple Node.js server running on Windows 10 side and I can easily access the server using the loopback address from inside WSL2 with a simple "curl" command as shown in Figure 5-19.

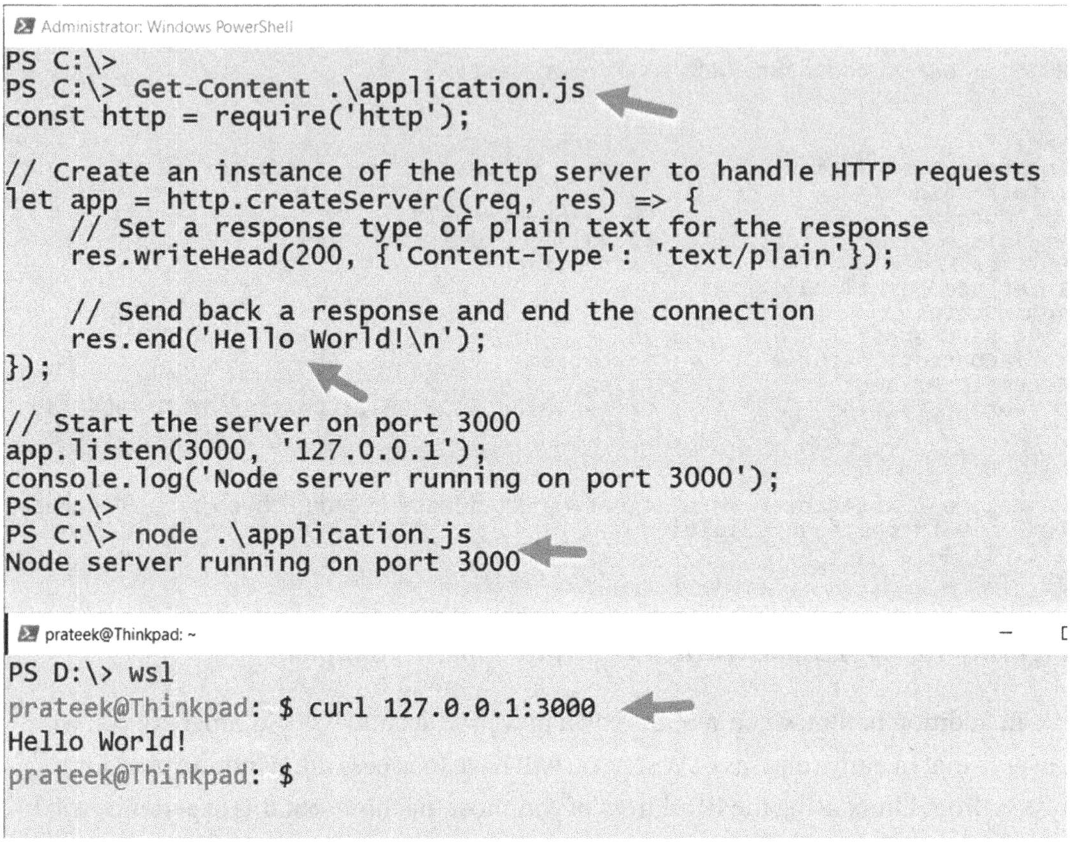

```
Administrator: Windows PowerShell
PS C:\>
PS C:\> Get-Content .\application.js
const http = require('http');

// Create an instance of the http server to handle HTTP requests
let app = http.createServer((req, res) => {
    // Set a response type of plain text for the response
    res.writeHead(200, {'Content-Type': 'text/plain'});

    // Send back a response and end the connection
    res.end('Hello World!\n');
});

// Start the server on port 3000
app.listen(3000, '127.0.0.1');
console.log('Node server running on port 3000');
PS C:\>
PS C:\> node .\application.js
Node server running on port 3000
```

```
prateek@Thinkpad: ~                                          —   口
PS D:\> wsl
prateek@Thinkpad: $ curl 127.0.0.1:3000
Hello World!
prateek@Thinkpad: $
```

Figure 5-19. *Accessing a Node.js server on Windows from WSL2*

Accessing Linux Applications from Windows

Just like we accessed a Windows application from Linux in the previous example, similarly we can also access a Linux application, a Node.js server running in a WSL Linux distribution, on http://localhost from Windows 10 side. Figure 5-20 demonstrates a PowerShell Invoke-WebRequest command to access the endpoint running on WSL.

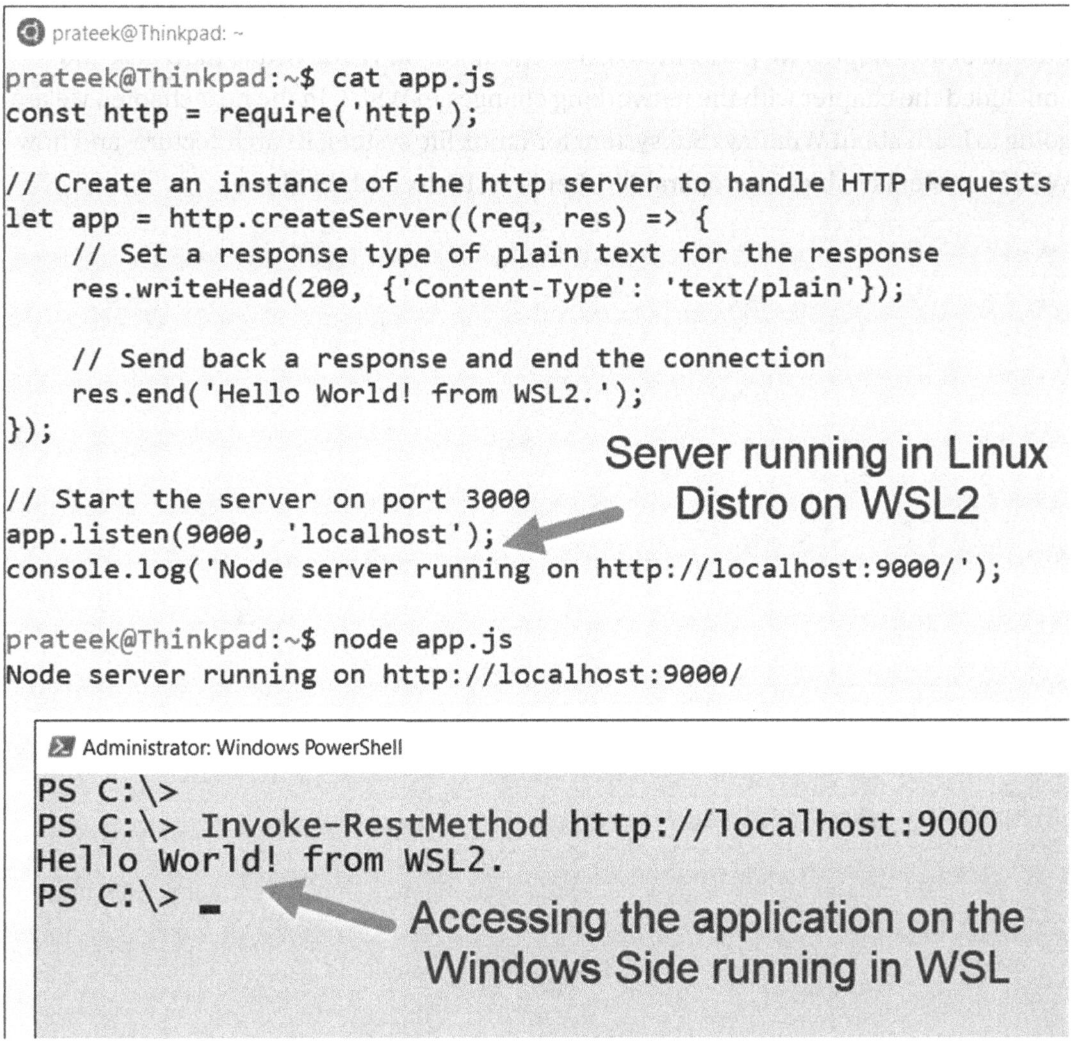

```
● prateek@Thinkpad: ~

prateek@Thinkpad:~$ cat app.js
const http = require('http');

// Create an instance of the http server to handle HTTP requests
let app = http.createServer((req, res) => {
    // Set a response type of plain text for the response
    res.writeHead(200, {'Content-Type': 'text/plain'});

    // Send back a response and end the connection
    res.end('Hello World! from WSL2.');
});
                                        Server running in Linux
// Start the server on port 3000         Distro on WSL2
app.listen(9000, 'localhost');◄
console.log('Node server running on http://localhost:9000/');

prateek@Thinkpad:~$ node app.js
Node server running on http://localhost:9000/
```

```
▨ Administrator: Windows PowerShell

PS C:\>
PS C:\> Invoke-RestMethod http://localhost:9000
Hello World! from WSL2.
PS C:\> ▬        Accessing the application on the
                 Windows Side running in WSL
```

Figure 5-20. *Accessing a Node.js server on WSL2 from Windows*

Summary

In this chapter, we learned new features and improvements in WSL2 and the purpose behind shipping a full Linux kernel to Windows 10 to support a new version of the Windows Subsystem for Linux. We enabled and performed the installation of WSL2 and learned to run WSL1 and WSL2 subsystem platforms in parallel. Later, we also looked into converting a WSL1 Linux distribution to WSL2-compatible distro and then benchmarked the file system and network performance improvements in WSL2. Toward the end of the chapter, we performed resize operation on WSL2 virtual hard disk and concluded the chapter with the networking changes in WSL2. In the next chapter, we are going to learn about Windows Subsystem for Linux file system, its architecture, and how WSL file system enables interoperability between Linux and Windows.

CHAPTER 6

File System

In this chapter, we are going to learn about how file systems work seamlessly as if you are working on a Linux file in the Linux operating system and additionally enables developers and power users to use full Windows and Linux interoperability to enhance their productivity. Since its inception, one of the purposes of the Windows Subsystem for Linux was to bring the best of both worlds together and not isolate the Windows and Linux operating system from each other like a traditional virtual machine where you can only use network shares and some other solutions to access files between the host and guest operating systems. Instead, the goal was to integrate these in such a way that WSL can directly access Windows files and Windows can access files within a Linux distribution running on WSL.

Before we can dive further into file systems, let us first understand some basic components that make the Windows Subsystem for Linux's file systems work.

File System Components

To support a Linux file system running on top of Windows, the Windows Subsystem for Linux has to translate all the user operations performed on Linux file systems to NT kernel operations. Moreover, users should be able to access Windows files from the Linux distribution running on top of WSL.

© Prateek Singh 2020
P. Singh, *Learn Windows Subsystem for Linux*, https://doi.org/10.1007/978-1-4842-6038-8_6

VFS

In order to provide this, WSL has a VFS component built into lxcore.sys that is modeled to emulate the Linux operating system's Virtual File System (VFS). The role of VFS in the Linux operating system is to provide an abstraction layer to manage all the file systems mounted at any moment on Linux. This abstraction facilitates common operations (like open, read, chmod, stat) and implementations irrespective of the underlying file systems that can coexist. Some of these file systems are as follows:

- volfs
- drvfs
- tmpfs
- procfs
- sysfs

Let's look into each of these separately.

volfs

This is the primary file system on WSL that is used to store all Linux system files and your home directory and almost has feature parity with the Linux Virtual File System (VFS). Technically, all files are on Windows, and WSL provides full access to these files by emulating the Linux behavior for internal Linux file systems, like the following directories which are added to each Linux distribution:

- /
- /root
- /home

But the purpose of this file system is not interoperability, but more of providing the Linux experience to the user which they are familiar with, like the /home or /root directories. That being mentioned, if a new file is added from the Windows side, it doesn't have the right extended attributes that are understood by volfs and they are simply ignored, and such files become unusable for the Linux distribution in the Windows Subsystem for Linux.

Let's take an example of file creation from Windows to this file system to understand it better. In the first approach, we attempt to create a file in the /home/prateek directory in the %LocalAppData%\ folder on my Windows 10 machine where all the package files for my Ubuntu 18.04 Linux distribution are placed.

Please note that the first approach is not a recommended way to add a file to your Linux distribution on WSL and may lead to file corruption and discrepancies. It is advised to not touch this folder from the Windows side:

```
$rootFS = "Packages\<package name>\LocalState\rootfs\home\<username>"
$param1 = @{
            ItemType = 'File'
            Path = "$env:LOCALAPPDATA\$rootFS\file1.txt"
}
New-Item @param1 -Verbose
```

When we run the preceding command from a PowerShell console on the Windows side, we see the file file1.txt has been created from the PowerShell console. The same can be verified from the %LocalAppData% folder. But if you closely observe in Figure 6-1, file1.txt is missing from the Ubuntu distro running on WSL.

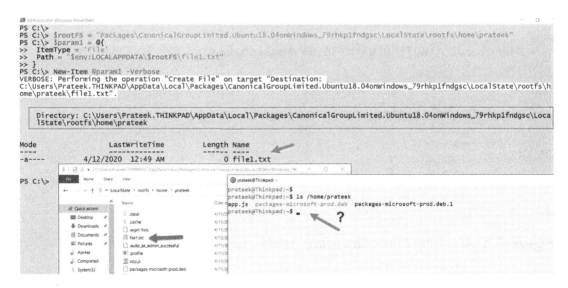

Figure 6-1. *Accessing Linux files from %LocalAppData% folder, not recommended*

On the other hand, when we create a file named "file2.txt" using the second approach, which is through the UNC path \\wsl$\ as demonstrated in Figure 6-2, using the following code sample, this not only creates the file but this file is now also available in the Windows Subsystem for Linux, unlike the first approach. Just to reemphasize, the second approach is the recommended method to create WSL files from Windows, and it is not a best practice to create or edit files from Linux packages placed in %LocalAppData% folder:

```
$param2 = @{
        ItemType = 'File'
        Path = \\wsl$\Ubuntu-18.04\home\prateek\file2.txt
}
New-Item @param2 -Verbose
```

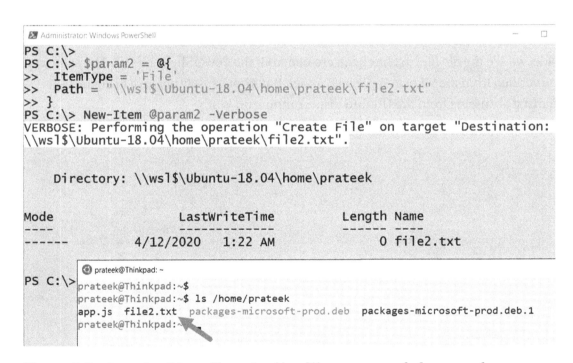

Figure 6-2. *Accessing Linux files using \\wsl$\, recommended approach*

The creation of files using the UNC path \\WSL$\<package>\ works because the Windows Subsystem for Linux adds some extended attributes using this method on the files created, and Figure 6-3 demonstrates this extended attribute (EA) being slapped on "file2.txt" but is missing from the "file1.txt" when examined through "fsutil.exe".

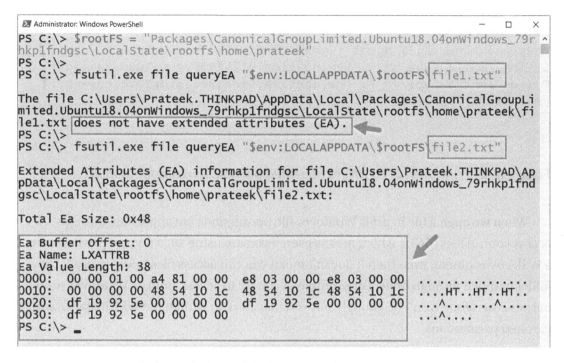

Figure 6-3. *Extended attributes added to NTFS files to appear in WSL*

drvfs

This file system is automatically mounted on Linux distributions to provide interoperability with Windows, so that drives mounted on the NT file system are accessible from the Windows Subsystem for Linux as shown in Figure 6-4. drvfs currently only supports New Technology File System (NTFS) and Microsoft's newest file system, the Resilient File System (ReFS). The Windows Subsystem for Linux will automatically mount fixed drives under the /mnt folder as

- /mnt/c
- /mnt/d

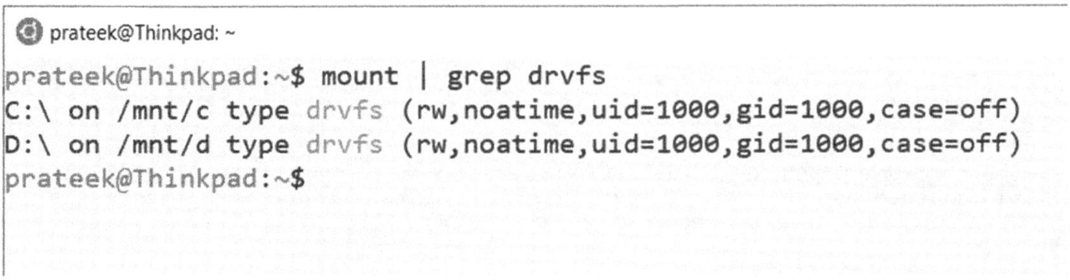

```
🌀 prateek@Thinkpad: ~

prateek@Thinkpad:~$ mount | grep drvfs
C:\ on /mnt/c type drvfs (rw,noatime,uid=1000,gid=1000,case=off)
D:\ on /mnt/d type drvfs (rw,noatime,uid=1000,gid=1000,case=off)
prateek@Thinkpad:~$
```

Figure 6-4. *Windows NTFS drives mounted on WSL as drvfs file system*

When we open a file in drvfs Windows, file permissions are applicable through access control lists (ACL), which means even if you are using sudo for root privileges in a WSL environment, even then it doesn't mean you can access files under every NTFS folder mapped through drvfs. For example, if you try to access /mnt/c/Windows, sudo permissions alone won't be enough and you may have to launch the WSL instance with elevated permissions.

tmpfs

Everything in tmpfs is temporary in the sense that no files are created on your persistent storage such as your hard drive. Instead, all files are kept in volatile storage such as virtual memory. That means if you unmount a tmpfs, then everything stored inside it will be lost.

tmpfs uses a combination of memory (RAM) and disk-based swap space to create a file system, and since it uses RAM, it is very fast to read and write data compared to writing to a disk. There are multiple directories that are mounted using this file system like /dev and /run as seen in Figure 6-5.

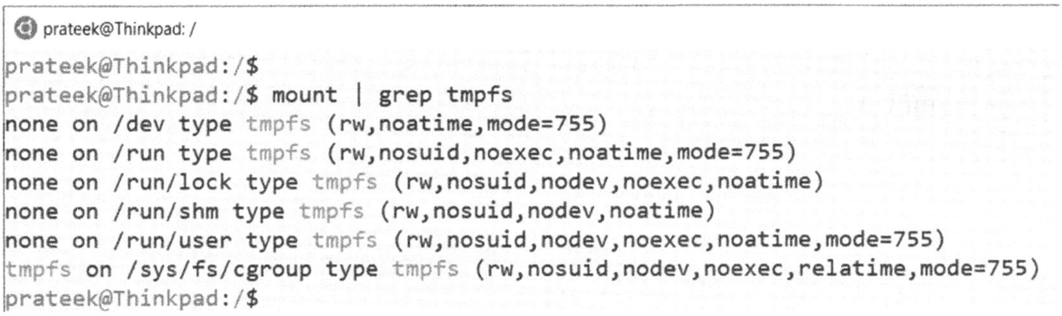

```
🌀 prateek@Thinkpad: /

prateek@Thinkpad:/$
prateek@Thinkpad:/$ mount | grep tmpfs
none on /dev type tmpfs (rw,noatime,mode=755)
none on /run type tmpfs (rw,nosuid,noexec,noatime,mode=755)
none on /run/lock type tmpfs (rw,nosuid,nodev,noexec,noatime)
none on /run/shm type tmpfs (rw,nosuid,nodev,noatime)
none on /run/user type tmpfs (rw,nosuid,nodev,noexec,noatime,mode=755)
tmpfs on /sys/fs/cgroup type tmpfs (rw,nosuid,nodev,noexec,relatime,mode=755)
prateek@Thinkpad:/$
```

Figure 6-5. *tmpfs is a temporary file system*

procfs, sysfs

procfs and sysfs are special file systems that represent system information like CPU, processes, drivers, devices, and configurations that are mostly dynamically generated when it is read. In the background WSL queries this information from the Windows NT kernel without any interaction with NTFS.

procfs is the earlier implementation where most of the system-related information can be found at the directory /proc, as shown in Figure 6-6 and the following examples where we can check the system uptime using

```
cat /proc/uptime
and verify the Linux kernel version:
cat /proc/version
```

```
🌀 prateek@Thinkpad: /                                                 —    □    ⟩
prateek@Thinkpad:/$
prateek@Thinkpad:/$ ls /proc/
1     8    bus      cpuinfo      loadavg  net   sys   version
211   98   cgroups  filesystems  meminfo  self  tty   version_signature
7     99   cmdline  interrupts   mounts   stat  uptime
prateek@Thinkpad:/$ cat /proc/uptime
24553.45 269647.96
prateek@Thinkpad:/$ cat /proc/version
Linux version 4.4.0-19041-Microsoft (Microsoft@Microsoft.com) (gcc version 5.4.0 (GCC) )
#1-Microsoft Fri Dec 06 14:06:00 PST 2019
prateek@Thinkpad:/$
```

Figure 6-6. *Accessing system information through /proc file system*

Since Linux kernel version 2.6, a new file system was implemented called sysfs that represents information at /sys in a more structured and easily searchable manner. /sys can be utilized to get information like power settings or the physical address of an Ethernet port as demonstrated in Figure 6-7.

```
● prateek@Thinkpad: /
prateek@Thinkpad:/$
prateek@Thinkpad:/$ ls /sys/
block  bus  class  dev  devices  firmware  fs  kernel  module  power
prateek@Thinkpad:/$ cat /sys/power/autosleep
off
prateek@Thinkpad:/$ ls /sys/class/
backlight  net  power_supply  switch  timed_output
prateek@Thinkpad:/$ ls /sys/class/net/
eth0  eth1  eth2  eth3  eth4  lo  wifi0  wifi1
prateek@Thinkpad:/$ cat /sys/class/net/eth0/address
48:2a:e3:41:fc:ad
prateek@Thinkpad:/$ ▂
```

Figure 6-7. *Accessing system information through the /sys file system*

Multiple UNC Provider (MUP)

The multiple UNC provider (MUP) is a kernel-mode component part of the mup.sys binary that is responsible for redirecting any UNC-based remote file system access to a network redirector (the UNC provider) that can fulfill such file system requests.

Basically, the MUP determines which provider can handle a UNC path in a name-based operation, and this is also known as "prefix resolution." As shown in Figure 6-8, the order in which these network providers are queried for prefix resolution is based on the comma-separated value for the following registry entry:

```
$path = 'HKLM:\SYSTEM\CurrentControlSet\Control\NetworkProvider\Order\'
(Get-ItemProperty $path).ProviderOrder -split ','
```

```
▲ Administrator: Windows PowerShell
PS C:\>
PS C:\> $path = 'HKLM:\SYSTEM\CurrentControlSet\Control\NetworkProvider\Order\'
PS C:\> (Get-ItemProperty $path).ProviderOrder -split ','
RDPNP
LanmanWorkstation
webclient
P9NP
PS C:\>
```

Figure 6-8. *List of network providers for prefix resolution of UNC paths*

When a WSL instance is launched, an init process is initiated that sets up a 9P server on WSL and a Unix socket for communication, which then uses the LXSS Manager service to register the WSL package name, and a Unix socket to the 9P file server to the 9P redirector used by MUP.

So when a user from Windows attempts to access the \\wsl$\<packagename> UNC path for WSL file system, then under the hood MUP is working for prefix resolution and finally uses the P9NP (Plan 9 Network Provider) to connect to a 9P file server running on WSL to enable file operations and interoperability between the two systems.

9P (Plan 9 Protocol)

9P (or the Plan 9 File System Protocol) is a network protocol that is used to set up a 9 file server (on WSL) and a client (on Windows) to bridge the Windows and Linux file systems and provide seamless interoperability. There are various reasons why this protocol was used instead of using the SMB protocol, which is already very popular on the Windows operating system. Some of the reasons follow:

- There is the possibility that SMB may not be installed by default on your system.

- And it may already be configured and it is not very wise to run multiple SMB instances and overwrite the configuration.

- If a Linux distribution doesn't have Samba, it cannot be shipped by Microsoft as it is GNU GPL licensed and can't be shipped with Windows 10 operating system.

- SMB is complex and difficult to implement under the Windows Subsystem for Linux, compared to 9P which is simpler and straightforward.

WSL File System Architecture

Before we understand the file system architecture of WSL and how files are accessed from Windows to Linux and vice versa, let's first understand the setup workflow that is a requirement to make the interoperability between the file systems work through the following steps, and these steps are highlighted with light blue numbered labels in Figure 6-9:

1. The moment a WSL.exe instance is launched, it interacts with the
    LXSS Manager service.

2. LXSS.sys then communicates with the Windows Subsystem for
    Linux to run the init process.

3. This init process is also responsible to initialize the subsystem
    and set up a Plan 9 protocol file server in WSL.

4. This server will then coordinate with the LXSS Manager service to
    set up a Unix socket for the file system communication.

5. Once that is done, the Linux distribution's name and Unix socket
    is then registered to the 9P redirector to make it aware where to
    connect for any request resolving to UNC path
    \\wsl$\<packagename>.

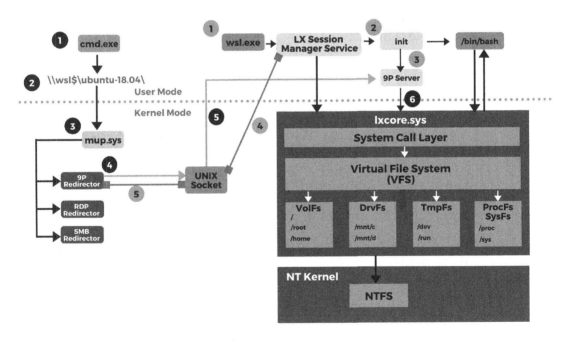

Figure 6-9. *WSL1 file system architecture*

Once this initial setup is complete, then the following steps are involved in order to
access a file from Windows to Linux operating system running over WSL:

1. A Windows process like CMD.exe or PowerShell.exe attempts to access Linux file on WSL using the UNC path \\wsl$\<packagename>.

2. This request is transferred to MUP (multiple UNC provider) which attempts to resolve this path and connect to the appropriate remote file system.

3. MUP achieves this by finding the network provider or the redirector that has been registered for such a type of request.

4. Since in the previous subsection a Unix socket was registered for WSL on 9P redirector to handle such requests, this socket will be utilized by MUP to create a 9P file server connection to the Linux file system on WSL.

5. Now this 9P server can communicate with lxcore.sys to facilitate any file system access or operations from Windows using the Virtual File System (VFS) and emulating the Windows system calls to Linux system calls.

Note   There is one major difference between the file system architecture of WSL1 and WSL2, and that is on WSL1 all the files are stored on Windows drives using NTFS, on contrary to that of WSL2 in which the Linux files are stored in a virtual hardware disk (VHD) using the ext4 file system.

Windows-Linux Case Sensitivity

Windows applications while creating files using the `CreateFile` API have the ability to pass a flag FILE_FLAG_POSIX_SEMANTICS which is an indication that case sensitivity is enabled for the file path. You can read more about this API and flag here: `https://docs.microsoft.com/en-us/windows/win32/api/fileapi/nf-fileapi-createfilea`. The Windows operating system has had this capability since Windows XP, but this is overridden by default through a global registry.

To support case-sensitive files used by Linux applications running on WSL, the Windows Subsystem for Linux has other mechanisms to bypass the global registry settings to set FILE_FLAG_POSIX_SEMANTICS flag to give users a case-sensitive experience just like Linux, but also makes the files accessible by Windows applications.

The Windows Subsystem for Linux uses another mechanism, which itself bypasses that registry key, allowing us to perform case-sensitive file system operations. This is what allows Linux applications running in WSL to use file names that differ only by case, just like they can on real Linux, even with that global registry key set. There is always the option to change the registry setting, but let's not forget that this is a global setting and changing it will change the case sensitivity for all drives, which may not be what we want and can lead to unintended behavior across applications or even break some other applications.

To overcome this drawback, a new case sensitivity flag was implemented to enable or disable case sensitivity on a directory level instead of a global setting and irrespective of the FILE_FLAG_POSIX_SEMANTICS flag on the files in this directory. This new flag allows two files in a directory to exist with the same name but with different cases still and be accessible to Windows applications.

Since Windows 10 build 17107, we can use fsutil.exe to view or modify this flag using the following command syntax:

```
fsutil.exe file queryCaseSensitiveInfo <directory path>
fsutil.exe file setCaseSensitiveInfo <directory path> <enable\disable>
```

Follow these steps to enable case-sensitive files using this fsutil.exe:

1. First thing first, launch a PowerShell console with administrative privileges and create a new directory, as this flag can be only applied on a directory level:

   ```
   mkdir testdir | Out-Null
   ```

2. Let's test the flag on the directory we just created in the previous step. By default case sensitivity is "disabled":

   ```
   fsutil.exe file QueryCaseSensitiveInfo D:\testdir\
   ```

3. Now, if we try to create two files with the same name but different cases, then the second command overwrites the first file and no second file is created, because case sensitivity is still not supported:

```
'test1' | Out-File D:\testdir\foo.txt
'test2' | Out-File D:\testdir\FOO.txt
ls D:\testdir\
```

4. Now, let's set the flag using fsutil.exe and re-attempt creating a file
    with the same name but different case:

    ```
    fsutil.exe file setCaseSensitiveInfo D:\testdir\ enable
    'test2' | Out-File D:\testdir\FOO.txt
    ```

5. This time a new file will be created as demonstrated in Figure 6-10,
    and you will be able to see both "foo.txt" and "FOO.txt" files in the
    directory irrespective of the case:

    ```
    ls D:\testdir\
    ```

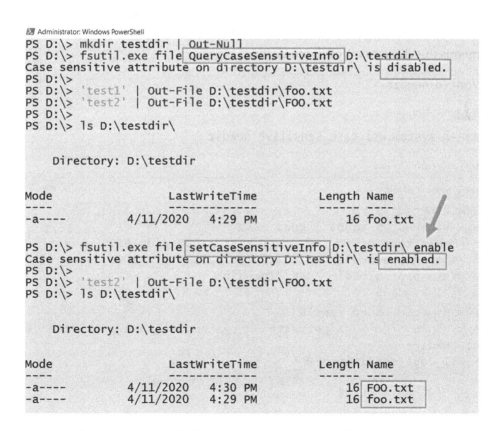

Figure 6-10. *Query and modifying case sensitivity attribute on NTFS*

With Windows 10 build 17692, tweaking case sensitivity was facilitated from within the Windows Subsystem for Linux through an extended attribute `system.wsl_case_sensitive` on a per-directory basis. To view or modify this extended attribute, we can use the `getfattr` and `setfattr` commands on Ubuntu, and you may need to install this using

```
sudo apt install attr
```

To enable this attribute, it is set to "1" and "0" disables the attribute.

The Windows Subsystem for Linux allows us to control case sensitivity on drvfs mount options using the `/etc/wsl.conf` file's [automount] section, and by default, these Windows drives mounted on WSL are case-insensitive. This means when case=off is set, then any new directories created on "drvfs" mounts will be case-insensitive.

Let's try this: when I check my mounted drives, I see by default `drvfs` is set to case=off:

```
mount | grep case
```

And when we create a new directory and check the `system.wsl_case_sensitive` extended attribute using `getdattr` as shown in Figure 6-11, we observe that it is set to "0" which means this directory is case-insensitive:

```
mkdir /mnt/d/newdir
```

```
cd /mnt/d/
getfattr -n system.wsl_case_sensitive newdir
```

Figure 6-11. *Query case sensitivity in WSL using "getfattr"*

So, if we attempt to create two files with the same name and different cases, then the first file will be overwritten by the second command and only one file will exist:

```
touch newdir/file.txt
touch newdir/FILE.txt
ls newdir/
```

To enable case sensitivity from inside WSL, we enable the extended attribute on the directory like in the following example:

```
setfattr --name system.wsl_case_sensitive --value 1 newdir
getfattr -n system.wsl_case_sensitive newdir
```

Now if we create a file with a different case, then both files will be created with the same name and different cases "file.txt" and "FILE.txt" as demonstrated in Figure 6-12:

```
touch newdir/FILE.txt
ls newdir/
```

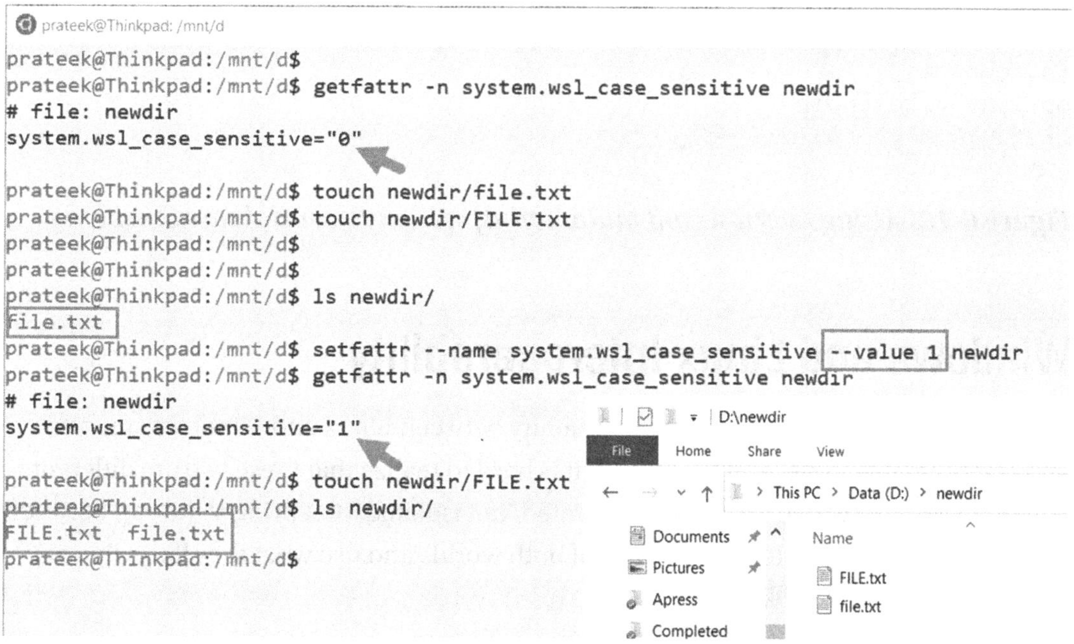

Figure 6-12. *Modifying case sensitivity per directory in WSL using "setfattr"*

The Windows Subsystem for Linux also allows to set mount options in /etc/wsl.conf file to case=dir, which means all new directories created will by default have case sensitivity enabled. This is demonstrated in Figure 6-13.

```
  prateek@Thinkpad: /mnt/d
prateek@Thinkpad:/mnt/d$
prateek@Thinkpad:/mnt/d$ mount | grep case
C:\ on /mnt/c type drvfs (rw,noatime,uid=1000,gid=1000,case=dir)
D:\ on /mnt/d type drvfs (rw,noatime,uid=1000,gid=1000,case=dir)
prateek@Thinkpad:/mnt/d$
prateek@Thinkpad:/mnt/d$ mkdir /mnt/d/mydir
prateek@Thinkpad:/mnt/d$ getfattr -n system.wsl_case_sensitive mydir
# file: mydir
system.wsl_case_sensitive="1"

prateek@Thinkpad:/mnt/d$ touch mydir/foo.txt
prateek@Thinkpad:/mnt/d$ touch mydir/FOO.txt
prateek@Thinkpad:/mnt/d$
prateek@Thinkpad:/mnt/d$ ls mydir/
FOO.txt  foo.txt
prateek@Thinkpad:/mnt/d$ cat /etc/wsl.conf
[automount]
options = case=dir
prateek@Thinkpad:/mnt/d$ 
```

Figure 6-13. *Using /etc/wsl.conf [automount] section to control case sensitivity*

Windows and Linux Interoperability

Microsoft has made file system interoperability between Linux and Windows smoother and smoother over time, and sometimes it is hard to realize that these two are different operating systems which are highly integrated, not isolated, that bridges the gap between them and enables users to pick the best of both worlds and use what they like, where they like, and how they like.

Accessing Windows Files from Linux

The drvfs file system mounted on the Windows Subsystem for Linux serves a major role to provide access to files on your Windows 10, so any fixed drives mounted on an NT file system are mounted on WSL. For example, the C:\ drive in NTFS will be available in the WSL as /mnt/c/ and similarly D:\ as /mnt/d/.

For example, as shown in Figure 6-14, we can list the contents of the directories using the ls command and the path /mnt/d/<path to directory>, and it will list all Windows files from the Windows Subsystem for Linux.

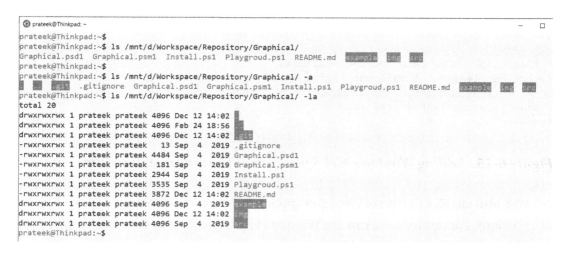

Figure 6-14. *Accessing Windows files from WSL using drvfs file system*

Additionally, we can also read the contents of these Windows files and even use our favorite Linux editor, such as nano, to edit files residing on an NT file system on Windows 10 as demonstrated in Figure 6-15.

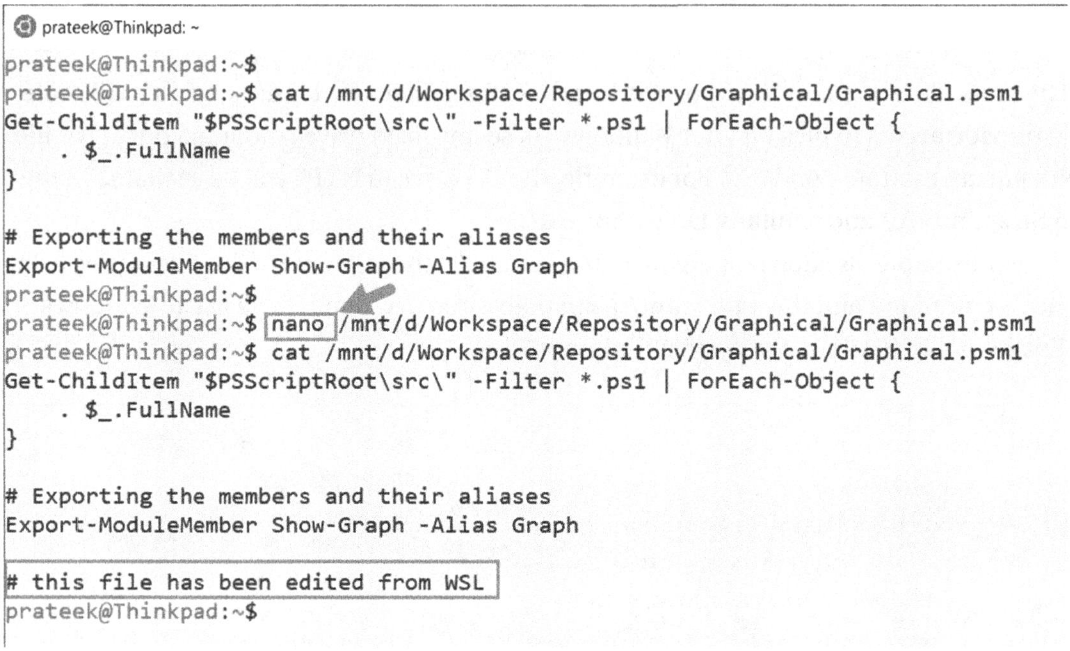

```
🟢 prateek@Thinkpad: ~
prateek@Thinkpad:~$
prateek@Thinkpad:~$ cat /mnt/d/Workspace/Repository/Graphical/Graphical.psm1
Get-ChildItem "$PSScriptRoot\src\" -Filter *.ps1 | ForEach-Object {
    . $_.FullName
}

# Exporting the members and their aliases
Export-ModuleMember Show-Graph -Alias Graph
prateek@Thinkpad:~$
prateek@Thinkpad:~$ nano /mnt/d/Workspace/Repository/Graphical/Graphical.psm1
prateek@Thinkpad:~$ cat /mnt/d/Workspace/Repository/Graphical/Graphical.psm1
Get-ChildItem "$PSScriptRoot\src\" -Filter *.ps1 | ForEach-Object {
    . $_.FullName
}

# Exporting the members and their aliases
Export-ModuleMember Show-Graph -Alias Graph

# this file has been edited from WSL
prateek@Thinkpad:~$
```

Figure 6-15. *Editing Windows NTFS files from WSL using a Linux editor*

WSL also enables the use of Windows applications to access files from Linux distributions. For instance, we can use Windows File Explorer (explorer.exe) to open the current working directory from a WSL console.

As you can see in the following example, we were able to launch our current working directory, that is, /home/prateek/, in explorer as a UNC-based shared path \\wsl$\Ubuntu-18.04\ home\prateek\ highlighted in Figure 6-16. Here I can move, edit, and perform all sorts of file operations, and these changes will reflect back in our Linux distribution running on WSL.

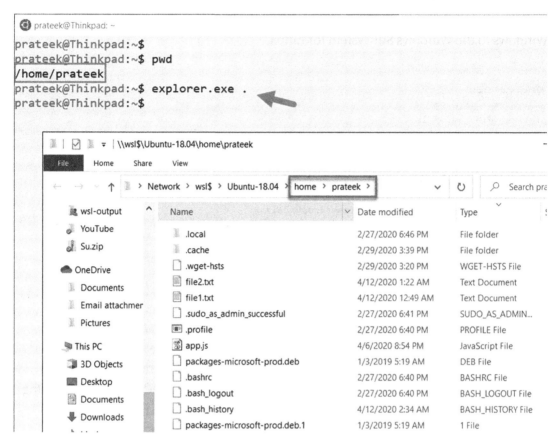

Figure 6-16. *Using Windows Explorer.exe for Linux files from WSL*

Linux commands like cp used to copy files can be used with drvfs mounts to access Windows NTFS drives and copy files into Linux as demonstrated in Figure 6-17.

```
prateek@Thinkpad: ~
prateek@Thinkpad:~$
prateek@Thinkpad:~$ ls
app.js  file1.txt  file2.txt  packages-microsoft-prod.deb  packages-microsoft-prod.d
prateek@Thinkpad:~$ cp /mnt/d/Workspace/input.json /home/prateek
prateek@Thinkpad:~$
prateek@Thinkpad:~$ ls
app.js  file1.txt  file2.txt  input.json  packages-microsoft-prod.deb  packages-micr
prateek@Thinkpad:~$
```

Figure 6-17. *Copying Windows files to WSL using drvfs file system*

Or as shown in Figure 6-18, use the mv command to move files or folders from Windows to the Windows Subsystem for Linux.

```
  prateek@Thinkpad: ~
prateek@Thinkpad:~$
prateek@Thinkpad:~$ ls
app.js  file1.txt  file2.txt  input.json  packages-microsoft-prod.deb  packages-microsoft
prateek@Thinkpad:~$
prateek@Thinkpad:~$ mv /mnt/d/Workspace/Repository/Graphical/ /home/prateek/
prateek@Thinkpad:~$
prateek@Thinkpad:~$ ls /home/prateek/
Graphical  app.js  file1.txt  file2.txt  input.json  packages-microsoft-prod.deb  package
prateek@Thinkpad:~$ ls /home/prateek/Graphical/
Graphical.psd1  Graphical.psm1  Install.ps1  Playgroud.ps1  README.md  example  img  src
prateek@Thinkpad:~$
prateek@Thinkpad:~$ ls /mnt/d/Workspace/Repository/Graphical/
ls: cannot access '/mnt/d/Workspace/Repository/Graphical/': No such file or directory
prateek@Thinkpad:~$
```

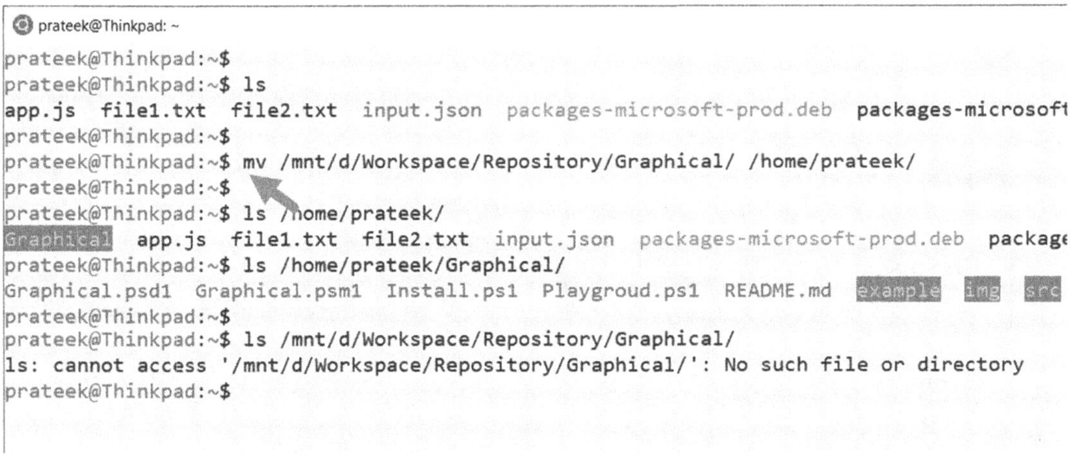

Figure 6-18. *Moving Windows files to WSL using drvfs file system*

The best part is that WSL gives us the ability to mix and match commands across operating systems, further bridging the gap between Linux and Windows. In the following example as demonstrated in Figure 6-19, I used ipconfig.exe, which is a Windows executable, to get the IP configuration from Windows in WSL, then filtered the output using the grep command which is a Linux command, and then again saved the file with the selected result to the Windows NT file system using drvfs mount option /mnt/ on the Windows Subsystem for Linux. I mean how cool is that and such a level of flexibility integrating the best of both worlds is hard to find:

```
ipconfig.exe | grep IPv4 > /mnt/d/ipaddress.txt
cat  /mnt/d/ipaddress.txt
```

```
● prateek@Thinkpad: ~
prateek@Thinkpad:~$
prateek@Thinkpad:~$ ipconfig.exe | grep IPv4
   IPv4 Address. . . . . . . . . . . . : 172.20.192.1
   IPv4 Address. . . . . . . . . . . . : 192.168.1.3
   IPv4 Address. . . . . . . . . . . . : 172.17.112.1
prateek@Thinkpad:~$
prateek@Thinkpad:~$ ipconfig.exe | grep IPv4 > /mnt/d/ipaddress.txt
prateek@Thinkpad:~$
prateek@Thinkpad:~$ cat /mnt/d/ipaddress.txt
   IPv4 Address. . . . . . . . . . . . : 172.20.192.1
   IPv4 Address. . . . . . . . . . . . : 192.168.1.3
   IPv4 Address. . . . . . . . . . . . : 172.17.112.1
prateek@Thinkpad:~$ ▄
```

Figure 6-19. *Using Windows executables with Linux commands*

Accessing Linux Files from Windows

Since the Windows Subsystem for Linux file systems are now highly integrated with Windows File Explorer (explorer.exe), all the Linux distributions are available at a special UNC path \\wsl$\ as demonstrated in Figure 6-20. I can see all Linux distributions and the files and folders they contain inside Windows File Explorer.

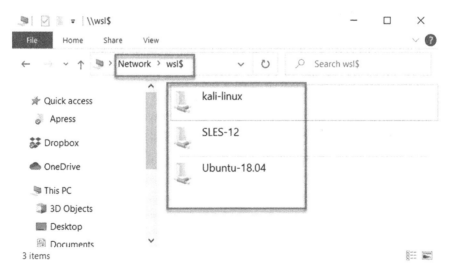

Figure 6-20. *Accessing Linux distribution file systems on UNC path: \\wsl$*

Please note that these paths for individual Linux distribution packages only appear if the Linux distribution is up and running. If the Linux distribution is not running on WSL, it won't appear at the \\wsl$\ UNC path.

So if you want to navigate to the Ubuntu file system from Windows, simply go to the address bar in File Explorer and type \\wsl$\Ubuntu018.04\ as demonstrated in Figure 6-21 and then hit Enter, and it will take you to the root directory of your Linux file system.

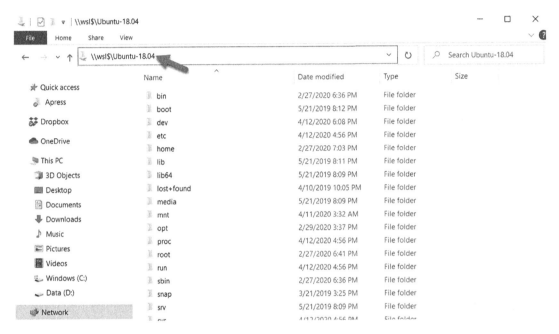

Figure 6-21. *Accessing specific Linux distro files using \\wsl$*

This \\wsl$\<disto-name>\ UNC path can be accessed to modify Linux files residing in your distro from CMD.exe or PowerShell.exe, and changes will be reflected in your Linux distribution. As demonstrated in the Figure 6-22, if we will create one file from the Windows Command Prompt and one from Windows PowerShell and place them both in my Linux distribution's home directory using the \\wsl$\ UNC path and then if we list the items in this folder, we can see both files with the right content from the WSL side.

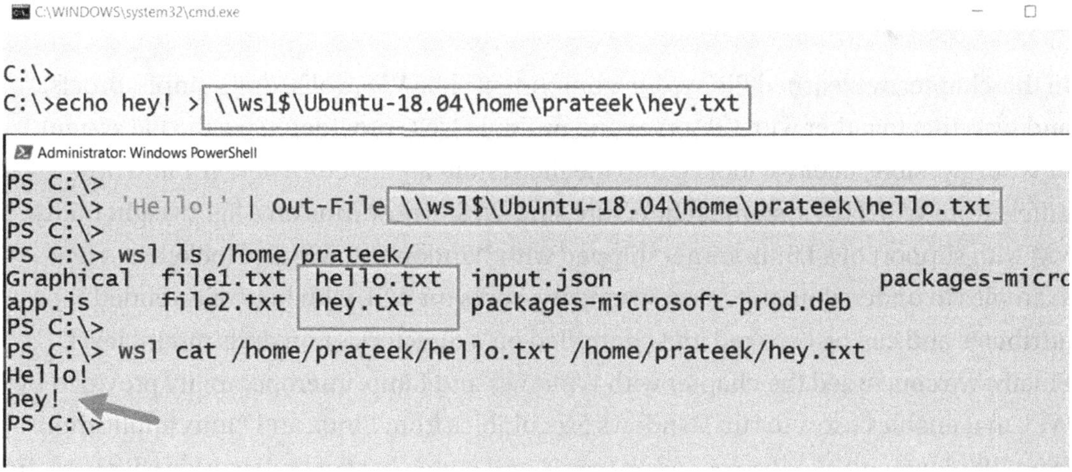

Figure 6-22. *Creating files on WSL using \\wsl$\ from Windows*

On top of that, you can also use the Windows Subsystem for Linux to run commands using wsl.exe and use the results in conjunction with CMD.exe commands like `findstr` and PowerShell cmdlets like `Select-String` to mix both the worlds together as shown in Figure 6-23 to improve user efficiency and get best of both worlds in one place.

Figure 6-23. *Running WSL and Windows commands in conjunction*

Summary

In this chapter, we learned file system components like VFS, volfs, drvfs, tmpfs, procfs, and sysfs that together with 9P server and multiple UNC provider make the file system of WSL1 possible; later we looked into the file system architecture of WSL1 and how it differs from WSL2 file system architecture since WSL2 now runs on a lightweight utility VM with support of a Linux kernel shipped with Windows 10. We also looked in a few examples to understand how case sensitivity works on WSL with help of extended attributes and can be tweaked and controlled on a directory or on drvfs mount level. Finally, we concluded the chapter with Windows and Linux interoperability provided by WSL that enables users to run Windows executables from Linux and Linux applications from Windows and allow power users to mix and match best of both worlds with ease. In the next chapter, we will learn WSl networking and how DNS and network interfaces are populated on the WSL side and the differences between WSL1 and WSL2 networking.

## CHAPTER 7

Networking

In this chapter, we are going to learn how the Windows Subsystem for Linux configures networking within the subsystem and how changes or updates in networking propagate from the Windows side to WSL. In addition, we will look into what Linux sockets are and how WSL implements them to provide a good Linux experience on top of the Windows operating system while maintaining interoperability.

Today, our computers are always connected to networks and devices, and we need constant access to the Internet and other systems through a network stack to exchange data, move files, and so on, further adding to the importance of networking as one of the crucial components behind the success of any software application.

WSL Networking Overview

Let's start with a small overview of how networking is set up on Linux and its implementation on WSL, and let us also discuss a little about design choices made to make a seamless compatibility layer to bridge the gap between Windows and Linux networking.

Network Interfaces and DNS

Linux uses generic system calls that can be utilized to control (read and write) any device like network interfaces, and such calls are also called Input/Output Control (IOCTL) . IOCTLs make it possible to view the list of all network interfaces connected to Linux, by making these syscalls to read the network interfaces and keeping this information in kernel. But WSL1 doesn't have this capability since there is no kernel available and we are actually emulating Linux over Windows using syscall translations on a compatibility layer.

© Prateek Singh 2020
P. Singh, *Learn Windows Subsystem for Linux*, https://doi.org/10.1007/978-1-4842-6038-8_7

In order to bridge this gap, as soon as a WSL instance is launched on Windows, the LXSS Manager service queries the list of the network interfaces on the Windows operating system and passes this list to the WSL driver (lxcore.sys), and whenever a system call (IOCTL) is made from a Linux distribution, then the aforementioned cached information provides the list of network interfaces in WSL.

The same list also gets auto-populated in the /etc/resolv.conf file, which is the resolver configuration file on Linux that contains the list domain name system servers configured on Windows. There are lots of configuration options that can be used in this file, but by default, it creates a common configuration:

```
nameserver <namer server IP address>
```

The IP address can be either an IPv4 address in dot notation or an IPv6 address in dot/colon notation, as demonstrated in Figure 7-1.

```
🌐 prateek@Thinkpad: ~                                           —    □    ✕
prateek@Thinkpad:~$ cat /etc/resolv.conf                             ^
# This file was automatically generated by WSL. To stop automatic generation of thi
s file, add the following entry to /etc/wsl.conf:
# [network]
# generateResolvConf = false
nameserver 192.168.1.1
nameserver fec0:0:0:ffff::1
nameserver fec0:0:0:ffff::2
prateek@Thinkpad:~$
```

Figure 7-1. *Auto-populated resolver file on WSL*

Some of this network query information also populates the /etc/hosts file also known as the host file, which contains a static lookup table of hostnames and their respective IP addresses as demonstrated in Figure 7-2. The combination of /etc/resolv.conf and /etc/hosts makes the DNS support possible on the Windows Subsystem for Linux.

```
 prateek@Thinkpad: ~                                               —    □    ×
prateek@Thinkpad:~$
prateek@Thinkpad:~$ cat /etc/hosts
# This file was automatically generated by WSL. To stop automatic generation of thi
s file, add the following entry to /etc/wsl.conf:
# [network]
# generateHosts = false
127.0.0.1       localhost
127.0.1.1       Thinkpad.localdomain     Thinkpad
172.20.2.207    host.docker.internal
172.20.2.207    gateway.docker.internal
127.0.0.1       kubernetes.docker.internal

# The following lines are desirable for IPv6 capable hosts
::1      ip6-localhost ip6-loopback
fe00::0 ip6-localnet
ff00::0 ip6-mcastprefix
ff02::1 ip6-allnodes
ff02::2 ip6-allrouters
prateek@Thinkpad:~$ _
```

Figure 7-2. *Auto-populated hosts file on WSL*

But networking is a very dynamic thing, and things change very quickly, for example, a user can very easily switch from wired Ethernet to a wireless network. There must be a mechanism in WSL to support updating these changes from Windows into WSL, so the LXSS Manager service again comes into the picture by registering itself for any notifications related to updates in network interfaces on the Windows side. That means the LxssManager service is listening for any update notifications, and if there is a change in networks, it will again be auto-populated into WSL using the aforementioned approach as demonstrated in Figure 7-3. This keeps the /etc/resolv.conf and /etc/hosts files up to date and synchronized with Windows configurations.

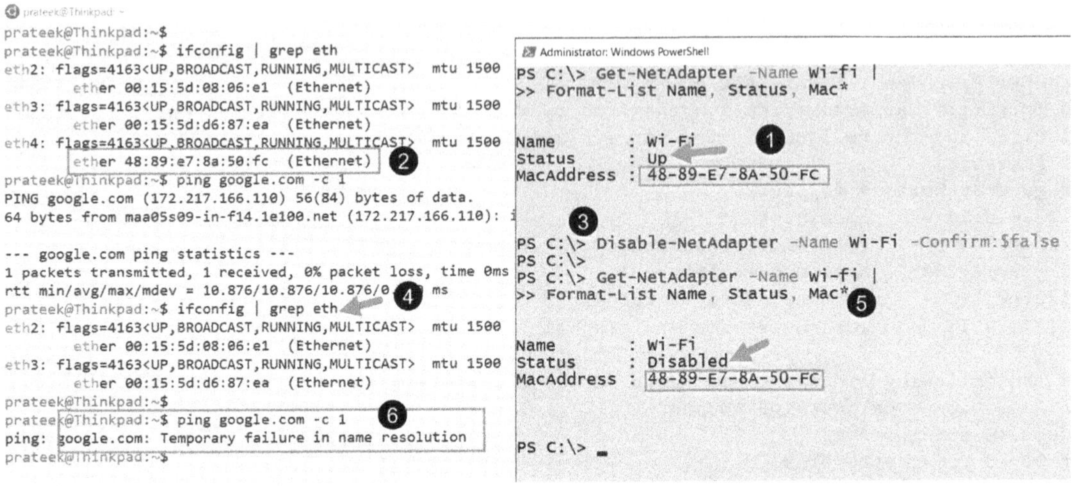

Figure 7-3. *WSL reconfigured by changes in the Windows environment*

Figure 7-3 demonstrates that in step 3 when the network interface is disabled on the Windows side, the Ethernet instantly disappears from the Windows Subsystem for Linux (verified through the missing MAC address in step 4), and ICMP requests start to fail at step 6.

Sockets

A socket is an abstract representation of an endpoint of a network communication path. Sockets can also serve as endpoints for local, non-networked inter-process communication. In the following subsection, we will cover a brief overview of Linux Berkeley sockets and similar implementation in Windows operating system called Winsock Kernel (WSK), which makes it possible for WSL to translate Berkeley socket API calls to Winsock Kernel API calls and vice versa to make networking possible between Windows and Linux.

Berkeley Sockets

In Linux, Berkeley sockets (also known as BSD sockets) is an API interface that allows inter-process communication (IPC). Any two endpoints, to establish communication, open a socket at each of their ends, which is then bound to a given address so that data can be sent or received between them.

Here are some of the common BSD socket API functions.

socket( )

It is used to create a new socket of a specific type and there are three requirements to open a socket, and they can further be used to categorize the socket:

1) **Address family (AF) or domain** – A socket can be one of these domains or address family.

   a) AF_INET is the Linux implementation of Internet Protocol version 4 (IPv4).

   b) AF_UNIX, also known as AF_LOCAL, is used for inter-process communication within the system.

   c) AF_NETLINK sockets are used for communicating between user mode and the kernel as they consist of a standard socket-based interface for user space processes and an internal kernel API for kernel modules.

2) **Socket type** – The socket type defines whether a protocol is connection-oriented or connectionless.

   a) SOCK_DGRAM for UDP

   b) SOCK_STREAM for TCP

   c) SOCK_RAW for ICMP

3) **Socket protocol** – The protocol argument can be set to zero "0" to request the default implementation of a socket type for the protocol.

   Syntax:

   ```
   socket(AddressFamily, Type, Protocol);
   ```

   Example:

   ```
   socket(AF_INET, SOCK_STREAM, 0);
   ```

bind( )

This function binds a socket with a socket address, that is, a combination of an IP address and a port number.

listen( )

This function marks the specified socket as a passive socket that will only accept incoming connections.

connect( )

This function is used to establish a connection between the referenced socket and passed IP address.

send( ), recv( ), sendto( ), and recvfrom( )

As the name suggests, these functions are used to send and receive data via sockets.

close( )

This function is used to release system resources by terminating a connection established through sockets.

Winsock and WSK (Winsock Kernel)

The Windows operating system has a user-mode implementation of the aforementioned BSD sockets known as "Winsock," and this implementation is very similar but not identical, and it couldn't be utilized in the Windows Subsystem for Linux because WSL's socket implementation is in kernel mode, that is within the Linux subsystem's driver library (WslSocket.lib).

To solve this challenge, another low-level Windows NT API, also known as Winsock Kernel (WSK), was used in WSL. WSK is a kernel-mode network programming interface, and using this, any kernel-mode software can perform network I/O operations just like user-mode "Winsock." Basically, Windows Subsystem for Linux drivers translate calls from BSD socket APIs to WSK APIs and implement whatever else is missing to support almost the same networking experience as there is on a native Linux distribution.

As demonstrated in Figure 7-4, when an application creates a BSD socket running in a Linux distribution on top of WSL, then BSD socket syscalls are made to the WSL's kernel-mode driver lxcore.sys, which handles the translation. lxcore.sys translates these BSD socket syscalls to calls that are understood by WSK (Winsock Kernel), which is a low-level API in the NT kernel to handle any socket-related requests on the Windows operating system and connect the socket to the underlying TCP/IP stack.

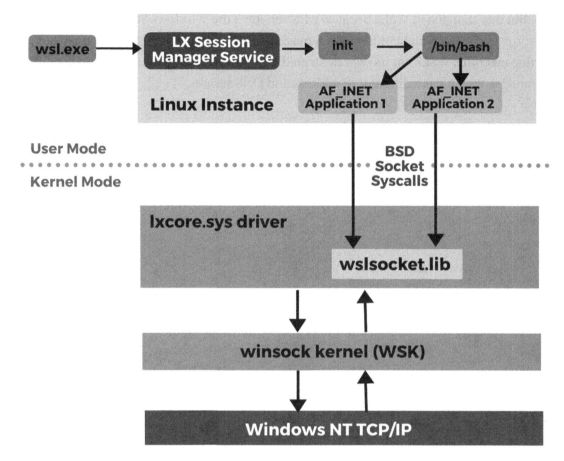

Figure 7-4. *WSL networking layout*

WSL vs. WSL2 Networking

How networking is implemented in Windows Subsystem for Linux versions 1 and 2 is totally different, and it is really important to understand the difference; otherwise, you will end up stuck with networking issues and unexpected behaviors.

One of the major differences is that in WSL1 the subsystem uses the same physical network interface used by the underlying Windows operating system, because everything else is just an emulation or in other words a compatibility layer built to support Linux distributions on Windows. That means you use the same Network Interface Cards (NICs), IP addresses, and DNS servers.

But this changed in WSL2 because with version 2 the Windows Subsystem for Linux now runs on a lightweight utility virtual machine built using Hyper-V, and just like any virtual machine, WSL2 has its own dedicated, virtualized network interface as shown in Figure 7-5, which has a different IP address and DNS servers.

```
Administrator: Windows PowerShell

PS C:\>
PS C:\> Get-NetAdapter *wsl* | Format-List


Name                        : vEthernet (WSL)
InterfaceDescription        : Hyper-V Virtual Ethernet Adapter #2
InterfaceIndex              : 61
MacAddress                  : 00-15-5D-D6-87-EA
MediaType                   : 802.3
PhysicalMediaType           : Unspecified
InterfaceOperationalStatus  : Up
AdminStatus                 : Up
LinkSpeed(Gbps)             : 10
MediaConnectionState        : Connected
ConnectorPresent            : False
DriverInformation           : Driver Date 2006-06-21 Version 10.0.19041.1



PS C:\>
```

Figure 7-5. *Virtual network to support lightweight VM for WSL2*

Apart from that, WSL1 and WSL2 both still populate /etc/resolv.conf and /etc/hosts files to make DNS resolution work, unless these files are explicitly overridden.

Summary

In this chapter, we learned the networking concepts behind the Windows Subsystem for Linux that makes the seamless experience and interoperability possible between Windows operating system and Linux subsystem. We covered network interfaces and how name resolution is set up and configured on WSL, and then we looked into Berkeley sockets and similar but not identical implementation in Windows called Winsock Kernel, which makes networking possible in the Windows Subsystem for Linux by translating the API calls. Finally, we covered the key difference in networking on WSL1 which emulates a Linux environment on Windows and WSL2 that is a lightweight utility virtual machine running over Windows operating system with a dedicated network interface.

## CHAPTER 8

Linux Development on WSL

Windows is a great platform and one of the most popular operating systems in the world, but we can't deny the sheer number of applications built and the workloads running on the Linux operating system. Microsoft has embraced this with the Windows Subsystem for Linux and other open source projects and other areas Microsoft has been contributing. In this chapter, we are going to learn about tools like VSCode and WSL remote extensions that enable developers to seamlessly develop Linux-based applications on the Windows operating system with all the necessary tools and runtime, in the comfort of your Linux environment running on top of the Windows Subsystem for Linux without worrying about Windows-Linux path translations, sharing files, or any other cross-operating system challenges.

Source Control

Before we can start setting up a Linux development environment on the Windows Subsystem for Linux, first we need to set up source control or version control to track and manage changes to our source code. Git is nowadays the most popular source control tool used by developers worldwide, so let's get started with setting it up.

Installing Git

Most of WSL distributions have "Git" pre-installed on them, but if it is missing or not installed by default like in kali-linux distribution, then you want to explicitly install "Git" on the Windows Subsystem for Linux by performing the following steps:

© Prateek Singh 2020
P. Singh, *Learn Windows Subsystem for Linux*, https://doi.org/10.1007/978-1-4842-6038-8_8

1. Launch WSL from the Windows Start menu. For this example, we
    are using Ubuntu 18.04.

2. In WSL, type the following command to install Git from the
    Ubuntu software repositories as shown in Figure 8-1:

    ```
    sudo apt-get install git
    ```

```
  ⊚ prateek@Thinkpad: ~
prateek@Thinkpad:~$ sudo apt-get install git
Reading package lists... Done
Building dependency tree
Reading state information... Done
Suggested packages:
  git-daemon-run | git-daemon-sysvinit git-doc git-el git-emai
The following NEW packages will be installed:
  git
0 upgraded, 1 newly installed, 0 to remove and 0 not upgraded.
```

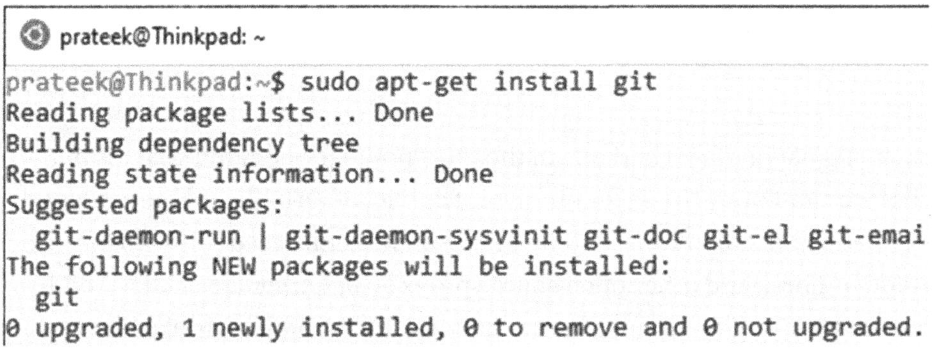

Figure 8-1. *Installing Git on WSL*

3. Now let's verify the version of the package installed by running
    the following command, and if you see version information like in
    Figure 8-2, then we are good to go.

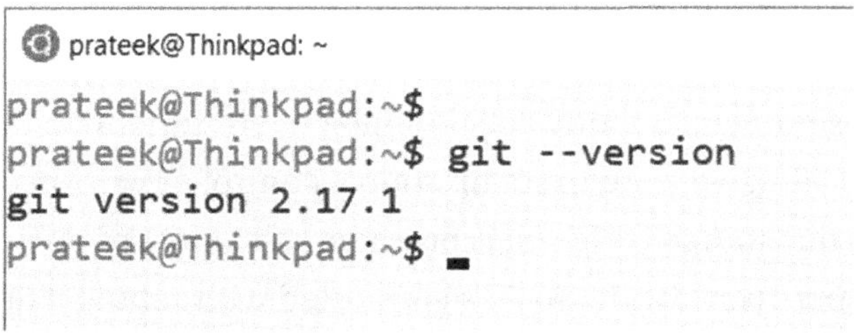

```
  ⊚ prateek@Thinkpad: ~
prateek@Thinkpad:~$
prateek@Thinkpad:~$ git --version
git version 2.17.1
prateek@Thinkpad:~$ ▄
```

Figure 8-2. *Checking Git version*

Setting Up and Configuring

First thing first, you need to set up an identity in Git, so that any change you make in the code is tagged with your name (Author's Name) and can be distinguished with any other code check-ins when you are working on a code repository with a team of developers:

```
git config --global user.name "Prateek Singh"
git config --global user.email prateek@ridicurious.com
```

Once the name and email are configured, you can list all the git configurations and verify them using `git config --list` as shown in Figure 8-3.

```
prateek@Thinkpad: ~
prateek@Thinkpad:~$ git config --global user.name "Prateek Singh"
prateek@Thinkpad:~$ git config --global user.email "prateek@ridicurious.com"
prateek@Thinkpad:~$
prateek@Thinkpad:~$ git config --list
user.name=Prateek Singh
user.email=prateek@ridicurious.com
prateek@Thinkpad:~$
```

Figure 8-3. *Setting global git configurations*

Resolving End-of-Line Differences in Windows and Linux

Since we are working in both Windows and Linux environments and files or programs you are editing can be created in Windows while you access them from WSL, some problems can appear. Because of the mix of these environments and the difference in default text line endings between Windows and Linux, you may see Git reporting a lot of modified files.

In order to demonstrate this, we checked in a Python file main.py in Windows using `git commit`. After that is done, there is nothing else to commit as we can determine from the result of command `git status`. Now when we open the same folder where the Python file was committed in the Windows Subsystem for Linux and run `git status`, it still shows uncommitted files. Upon checking the file difference using `git diff`, we see a strange character (^m) added at the end of the line as demonstrated in Figure 8-4; this is due to the line endings. Windows uses a carriage return and line feed (\r\n or CRLF)

as a line ending, whereas on Unix the ends of lines are represented with just a line feed
(\n or LF). The character ^M is the representation of a "carriage return" or CR so we
need to be very careful when transferring files between WSL (Unix) and Windows to
make sure the line endings are translated properly.

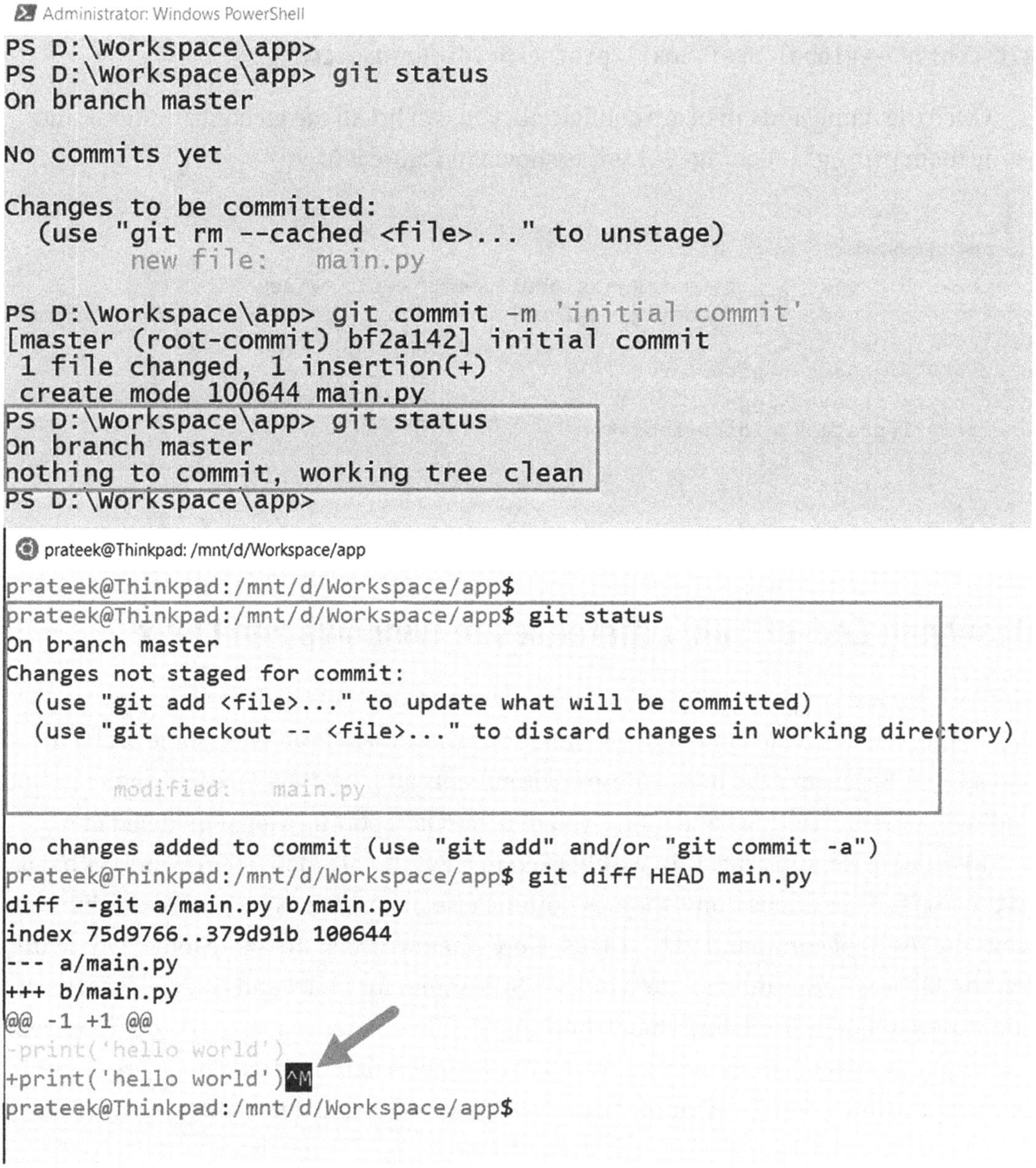

```
Administrator: Windows PowerShell
PS D:\Workspace\app>
PS D:\Workspace\app> git status
On branch master

No commits yet

Changes to be committed:
  (use "git rm --cached <file>..." to unstage)
        new file:   main.py

PS D:\Workspace\app> git commit -m 'initial commit'
[master (root-commit) bf2a142] initial commit
 1 file changed, 1 insertion(+)
 create mode 100644 main.py
PS D:\Workspace\app> git status
On branch master
nothing to commit, working tree clean
PS D:\Workspace\app>
```

```
prateek@Thinkpad: /mnt/d/Workspace/app
prateek@Thinkpad:/mnt/d/Workspace/app$
prateek@Thinkpad:/mnt/d/Workspace/app$ git status
On branch master
Changes not staged for commit:
  (use "git add <file>..." to update what will be committed)
  (use "git checkout -- <file>..." to discard changes in working directory)

        modified:   main.py

no changes added to commit (use "git add" and/or "git commit -a")
prateek@Thinkpad:/mnt/d/Workspace/app$ git diff HEAD main.py
diff --git a/main.py b/main.py
index 75d9766..379d91b 100644
--- a/main.py
+++ b/main.py
@@ -1 +1 @@
-print('hello world')
+print('hello world')^M
prateek@Thinkpad:/mnt/d/Workspace/app$
```

Figure 8-4. End-of-line differences in Windows and Linux

In order to resolve the line-ending issues using the following command on Windows, you can simply set the global git configurations to ensure the line endings in files you check out are correct for Windows and are also converted to Unix style when the files are committed:

```
git config --global core.autocrlf true
```

After making this global configuration change as demonstrated in Figure 8-5, the special character introduced because of "carriage return" appears to disappear on the Linux side while we are using the same Windows file. The file still contains the CR/LF characters, but now git understands to convert it to only LF end-of-line characters.

```
prateek@Thinkpad: /mnt/d/Workspace/app
prateek@Thinkpad:~$ cd /mnt/d/Workspace/app/
prateek@Thinkpad:/mnt/d/Workspace/app$ git status
On branch master
Changes not staged for commit:
  (use "git add <file>..." to update what will be committed)
  (use "git checkout -- <file>..." to discard changes in working directory)

        modified:   main.py

no changes added to commit (use "git add" and/or "git commit -a")
prateek@Thinkpad:/mnt/d/Workspace/app$ git config --global core.autocrlf true
prateek@Thinkpad:/mnt/d/Workspace/app$ git status
On branch master
nothing to commit, working tree clean
prateek@Thinkpad:/mnt/d/Workspace/app$ ▄
```

Figure 8-5. *Forcing CRLF end-of-line on WSL*

Sharing Git Credentials Between Windows and WSL

When you are working on both Windows and Linux, you also want your credentials to sync up; that means any credentials stored on Windows must be available to Git in the Windows Subsystem for Linux and vice versa.

If code repositories are cloned through HTTPS and you want credentials to persist between both Windows and WSL, then we need to perform the following steps to configure the Windows credential helper:

1. On Windows, open a PowerShell console and type the following command and hit Enter:

```
git config --global cretential.helper wincred
```

2. Now, we need to perform the same configuration on WSL, so we will launch a WSL instance and run the following command as shown in Figure 8-6, to point to the credential helper on Windows which we just configured, using the mounted drive at /mnt/c/:

```
git config --global credential.helper "/mnt/c/Program\ Files/Git/
mingw64/libexec/git-core/git-redential-wincred.exe"
```

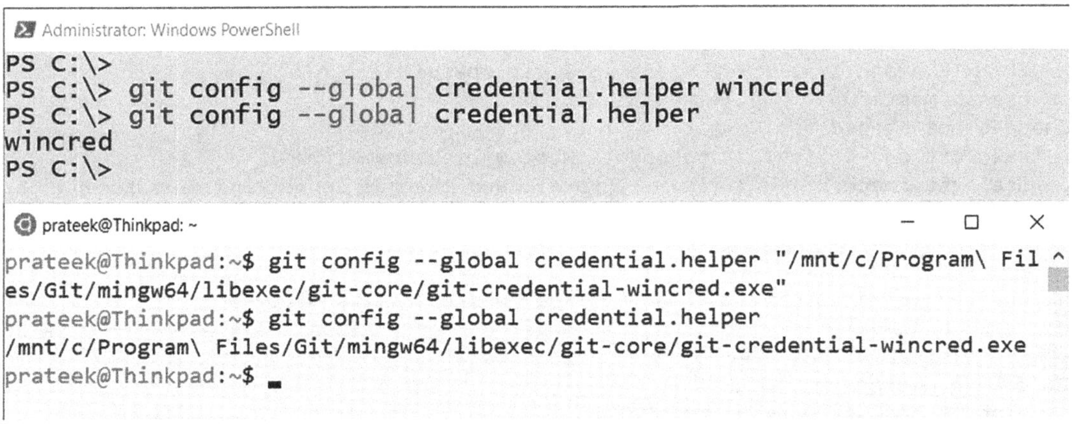

Figure 8-6. *Sharing git credentials with Windows Credential Manager*

When we use wincred as the credential.helper, git utilizes Windows Credential Manager to store your credentials, and with this configuration, it is accessible from both Windows and WSL.

Windows Terminal

Windows Terminal is an open source project by Microsoft that aims to deliver rich text-editing features, tab support, background, themes, and font styles. More than that, the new terminal provides key bindings and is highly configurable as settings are available in the form of a JSON file named settings.json.

The main purpose of the project was to provide an enhanced experience to developers on Windows, and it works very well with the Windows Subsystem for Linux by enabling developers to configure Linux distribution's command-line arguments to launch custom sessions. Before we jump into configuring WSL, let's quickly learn how to install Windows Terminal first, and there are two ways to achieve that.

Installing Windows Terminal from the Microsoft Store

Follow these steps to install Microsoft Terminal from the Microsoft Store:

1. Go to the Start menu at the bottom left of your Windows 10 screen and search for "Microsoft Store" and launch it as shown in Figure 8-7.

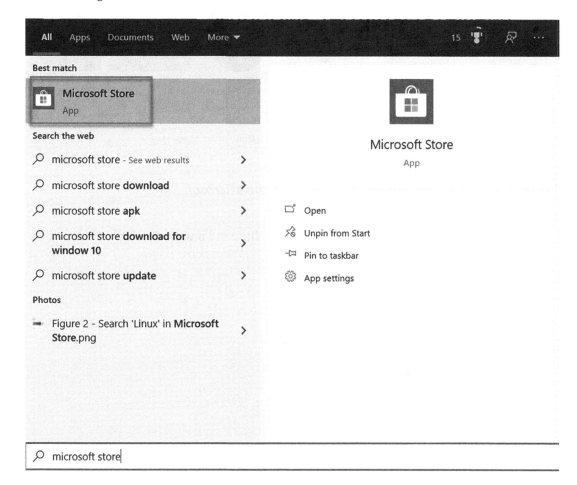

Figure 8-7. *Launch Microsoft Store*

2. Now in the Microsoft Store, search for "Windows Terminal", and
    from the results, click "Windows Terminal (Preview)", the one
    highlighted in Figure 8-8.

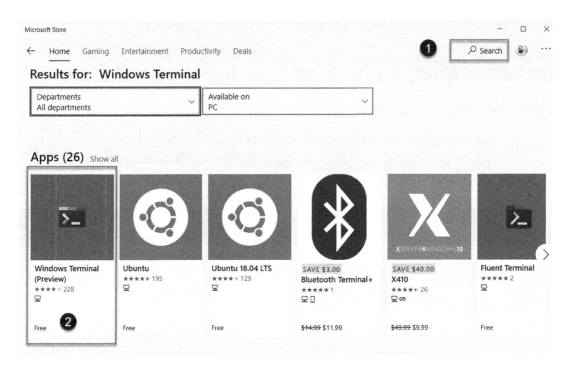

Figure 8-8. *Search for Windows Terminal in the Microsoft Store*

3. Then click the "Install" button as highlighted in Figure 8-9, which
    will start the download and installation.

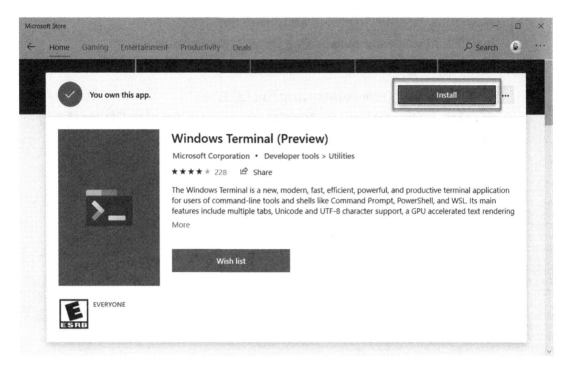

Figure 8-9. *Install Windows Terminal from the Microsoft Store*

4. Once the installation is complete, you can launch Windows
    Terminal from the Start menu.

Installing Windows Terminal Using Chocolatey

The second method is using the "Chocolatey" tool, which is a command-line installer for
Windows applications. Chocolatey uses the NuGet packaging format to package software
and applications by making them super easy to install on Windows.

Perform the following steps to install Chocolatey on Windows 10 and then install
Windows Terminal using that:

1. Launch a PowerShell console with administrative privileges.

2. Run the following command to make sure execution policies set
    on PowerShell don't hinder our installation:

```
Set-ExecutionPolicy Bypass -Scope Process -Force
```

3. Now using the following commands, we'll download the installation script and then use the Invoke-Expression cmdlet to run the script as demonstrated in Figure 8-10:

```
$URL = 'https://chocolatey.org/install.ps1'
$Script = (New-Object System.Net.WebClient).DownloadString($URL)
Invoke-Expression -Command $String
```

```
Administrator: Windows PowerShell
PS C:\> Set-ExecutionPolicy Bypass -Scope Process -Force
PS C:\> $URL = 'https://chocolatey.org/install.ps1'
PS C:\> $Script = (New-Object System.Net.WebClient).DownloadString($URL)
PS C:\> Invoke-Expression -Command $Script
Getting latest version of the Chocolatey package for download.
Getting Chocolatey from https://chocolatey.org/api/v2/package/chocolatey/0.10.15.
Downloading 7-Zip commandline tool prior to extraction.
Extracting C:\Users\PRATEE~1.THI\AppData\Local\Temp\chocolatey\chocInstall\chocol
TEE~1.THI\AppData\Local\Temp\chocolatey\chocInstall...
Installing chocolatey on this machine
Creating ChocolateyInstall as an environment variable (targeting 'Machine')
  Setting ChocolateyInstall to 'C:\ProgramData\chocolatey'
WARNING: It's very likely you will need to close and reopen your shell
  before you can use choco.
Restricting write permissions to Administrators
We are setting up the Chocolatey package repository.
The packages themselves go to 'C:\ProgramData\chocolatey\lib'
  (i.e. C:\ProgramData\chocolatey\lib\yourPackageName).
A shim file for the command line goes to 'C:\ProgramData\chocolatey\bin'
  and points to an executable in 'C:\ProgramData\chocolatey\lib\yourPackageName'.

Creating Chocolatey folders if they do not already exist.

WARNING: You can safely ignore errors related to missing log files when
  upgrading from a version of Chocolatey less than 0.9.9.
  'Batch file could not be found' is also safe to ignore.
  'The system cannot find the file specified' - also safe.
Chocolatey (choco.exe) is now ready.
You can call choco from anywhere, command line or powershell by typing choco.
Run choco /? for a list of functions.
You may need to shut down and restart powershell and/or consoles
  first prior to using choco.
Ensuring chocolatey commands are on the path
Ensuring chocolatey.nupkg is in the lib folder
PS C:\>
```

Figure 8-10. *Download Chocolatey Software*

4. Once the installation is complete, relaunch the PowerShell console and type choco --version. If you see version information, then we have a successful installation of Chocolatey.

After the installation of Chocolatey is complete on your machine, as demonstrated in Figure 8-11, we can proceed with installing Windows Terminal using the following command:

```
choco install microsoft-windows-terminal
```

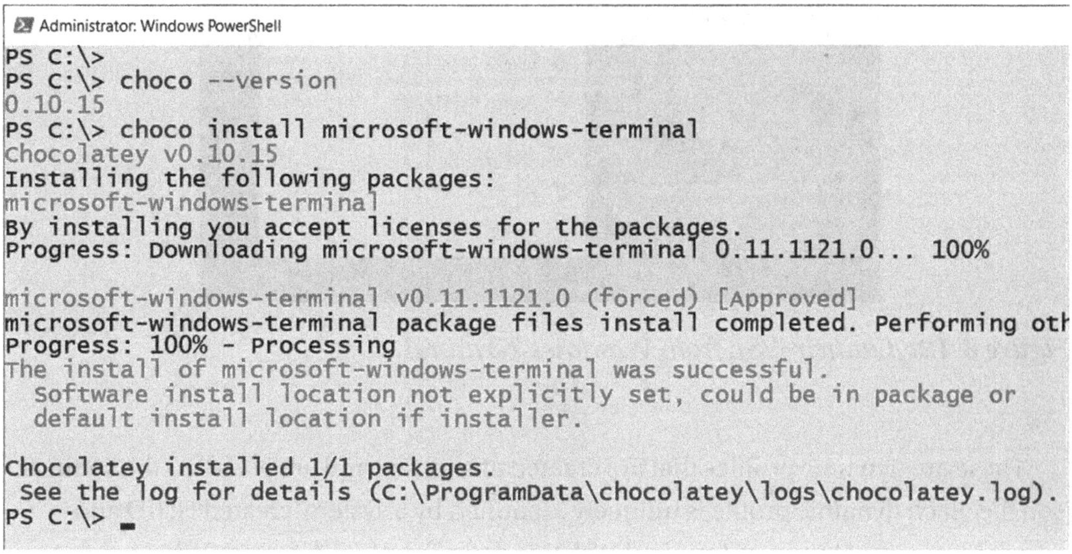

Figure 8-11. *Install Windows Terminal using Chocolatey*

Setting Up WSL in Windows Terminal

Now that we have installed Windows Terminal, let us go ahead and configure that with available Linux distributions for WSL. By default, all the Linux distributions are automatically populated under the down arrow sign in Windows Terminal as demonstrated in Figure 8-12.

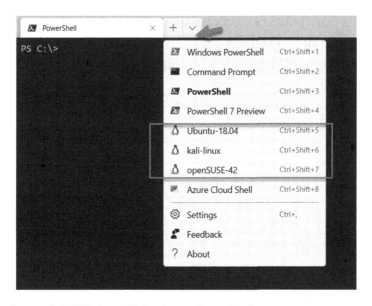

Figure 8-12. *Launch WSL from Windows Terminal*

These are dynamic profiles that are created at runtime and are added to the settings.
json file. Each dynamic profile is uniquely identified by a system-created GUID and
a source property: Windows.Terminal.Wsl, Windows.Terminal.Azure, or Windows.
Terminal.PowershellCore, something like the following sample:

```
{
    "guid": "{46ca431a-3a87-5fb3-83cd-11ececc031d2}",
    "hidden": false,
    "name": "Ubuntu-18.04",
    "source": "Windows.Terminal.Wsl"
}
```

We can also configure the settings.json file to run a custom-defined command-line
argument with WSL, for example, one that launches Ubuntu 18.04 in WSL as the "root"
user, as demonstrated in Figure 8-13. Windows Terminal settings are stored in settings.
json file which can be found at

%LOCALAPPDATA%\Packages\Microsoft.WindowsTerminal_8wekyb3d8bbwe\
LocalState\settings.json

```
{
    "guid": "{c6eaf9f4-32a7-5fdc-b5cf-066e8a4b1e40}",
    "hidden": false,
    "name": "Ubuntu-18.04",
    "commandline": "wsl.exe -u root -d ubuntu-18.04"
}
```

This setting can be also accessed from the Windows Terminal ➤ drop-down menu next to plus sign (+) for "New Tab" ➤ Settings. Or simply press keys Ctrl + to launch the settings.json file in the text editor.

Figure 8-13. *Adding WSL command line in Windows Terminal launch settings*

Figure 8-14 shows that you can also set the start directory of the Linux distribution and the session icon by providing paths as in the following example:

```
{
    "guid": "{c6eaf9f4-32a7-5fdc-b5cf-066e8a4b1e40}",
    "hidden": false,
    "name": "Ubuntu-18.04",
    "commandline": "wsl.exe -d ubuntu-18.04",
    "startingDirectory" : "D:\\Workspace\\",
    "icon" : "D:\\icon.jpg"
}
```

Note   In the preceding example, we escaped the backslashes in Windows file path, as backslash in Linux is used to mark the special characters.

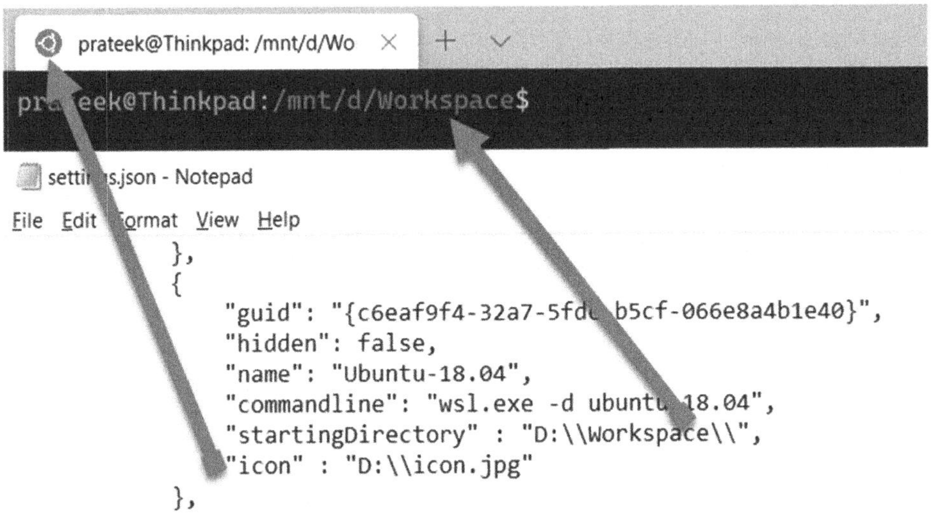

Figure 8-14.   *Adding icons and start directory for WSL in Windows Terminal*

There are lots of other configurations and settings available and can be found documented on GitHub where the Windows Terminal source code is available: https://github.com/microsoft/terminal.

Visual Studio Code (VSCode)

Visual Studio Code is a lightweight, powerful, and cross-platform code editor which can run on Windows, macOS, and Linux. VSCode supports a vast variety of programming languages like Python, C#, C++, PHP, and Java and is extensible through extensions that can be installed to extend the capabilities of the code editor.

The first step is to download and install Visual Studio Code from the following URL: https://code.visualstudio.com/download. This only takes a few minutes because of its lightweight nature. Once Visual Studio Code is installed, then we need to install the "Remote – WSL" extension.

The "Remote – WSL" extension enables developers to use the Windows Subsystem for Linux as the development environment for Visual Studio Code. That means WSL files are accessible to edit, and you can debug your Linux applications from Windows. This extension also takes care of a lot of path translations and compatibility issues between Windows and Linux.

VSCode sets up a VSCode server inside the Windows Subsystem for Linux, through which the tooling and frameworks running on Windows can be executed on WSL and a communication channel is set up that can take commands from Windows, and then execute them on WSL and return the output back to Windows.

Figure 8-15 demonstrates how Windows and WSL interact using Visual Studio Code.

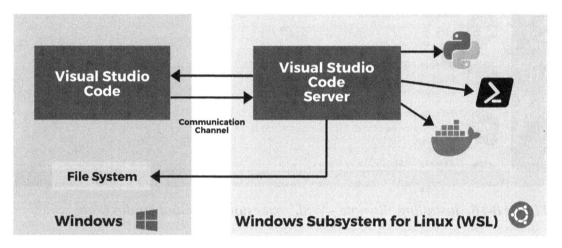

Figure 8-15. *Visual Studio Code remote server in the Windows Subsystem for Linux*

Installing the Remote - WSL Extension

1. Launch Visual Studio Code.

2. On the left sidebar, click the extensions icon and search for "Remote - WSL".

3. Now click "Install" on Remote – WSL extension by Microsoft as highlighted in Figure 8-16, and this will install the extension in VSCode.

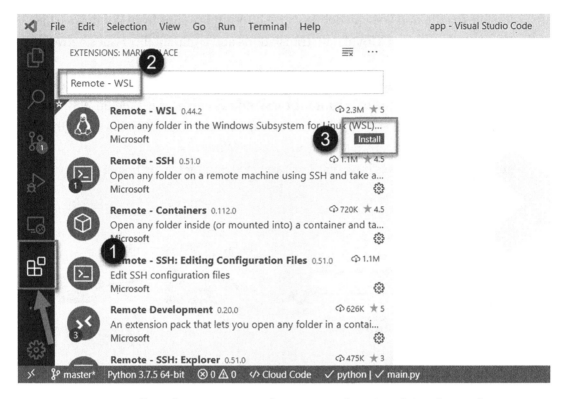

Figure 8-16. *Installing "Remote – WSL" extension for Visual Studio Code*

WSL Linux Distribution Support

Once the extension is installed, a new status bar item appears that can connect VSCode to the Windows Subsystem for Linux and also shows the current Linux distro to which Visual Studio Code is connected.

If we click this, it will launch a command palette with options to launch WSL instances in VSCode. If I choose the command "Remote-WSL : New Window", a new instance of Visual Studio Code will be launched and with the context of my default WSL Linux distribution, as can be seen in Figure 8-17.

Figure 8-17. *VSCode launched in context of WSL distro as seen from the bottom-left corner of IDE*

Since WSL supports more than one Linux distribution, we have another option from VSCode to support multiple Linux distributions; all you have to do is bring up the command palette (F1), search for "distro," and choose the command "Remote-WSL: New Window using Distro" as demonstrated in Figure 8-18.

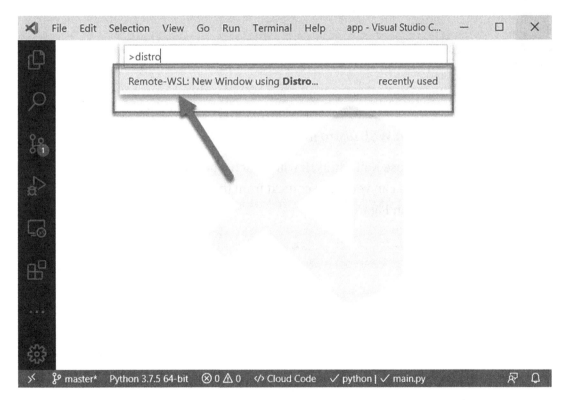

Figure 8-18. *Launching a WSL distro from Visual Studio Code*

This will then list all the current Linux distributions installed via the Windows Subsystem for Linux as shown in Figure 8-19 and lets you choose one to use with VSCode.

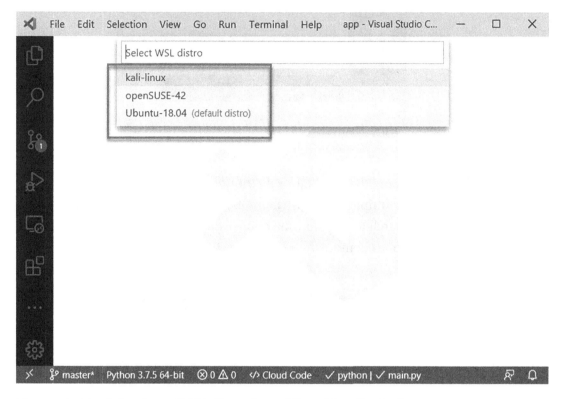

Figure 8-19. *Selecting a WSL distro from Visual Studio Code*

Let's suppose we choose Kali-Linux; it will launch a new VSCode instance with context of Kali-Linux. You can verify the context from the bottom-left corner of the Visual Studio Code highlighted in Figure 8-20.

Figure 8-20. *Visual Studio Code launched in context of chosen distribution*

Integrated Terminal and Default Shell

Once you are in the context of the Windows Subsystem for Linux, you can launch a new terminal from the menu bar, by left-clicking Terminal ▶ New Terminal as shown in Figure 8-21. Alternatively, you can also press Ctrl + to launch a new terminal.

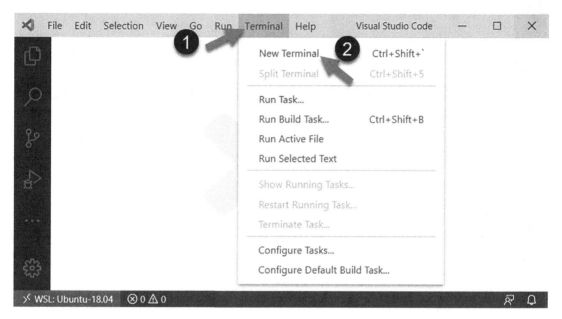

Figure 8-21. *Launching integrated terminal from VSCode's menu bar*

When the terminal is launched, it will automatically open the default shell in the Linux distribution we are working with as shown in Figure 8-22.

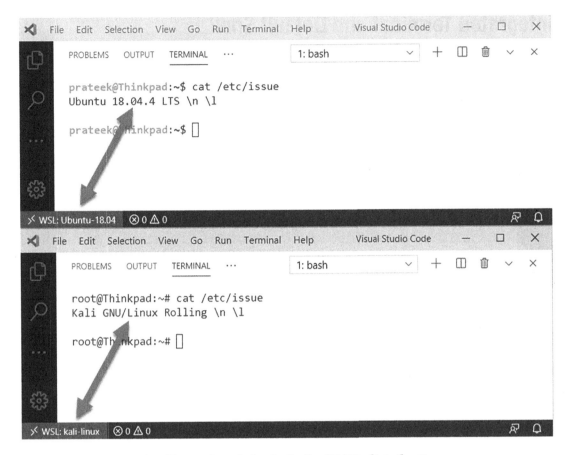

Figure 8-22. *Terminal launches default shell of WSL distribution*

Now that we are in the terminal with a bash shell inside a Windows Subsystem for Linux instance, we can set the default shell we want to launch every time the terminal instance is run. The following steps set up a default shell for WSL from VSCode running on Windows:

1. In the Visual Studio Code terminal launched in a WSL context, click the drop-down button on the right-hand side as shown in Figure 8-23.

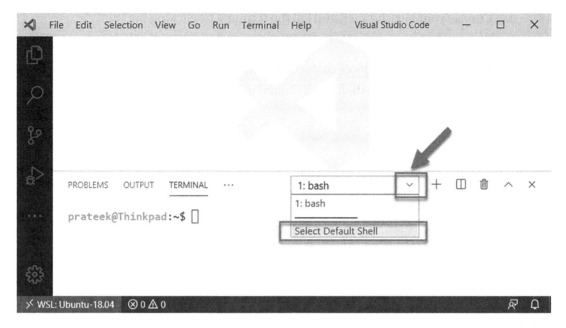

Figure 8-23. *Changing the default shell*

2. From the drop-down menu, click "Select Default Shell" as demonstrated in Figure 8-24. A command palette with a drop-down list of shell applications on your Linux distribution will pop up.

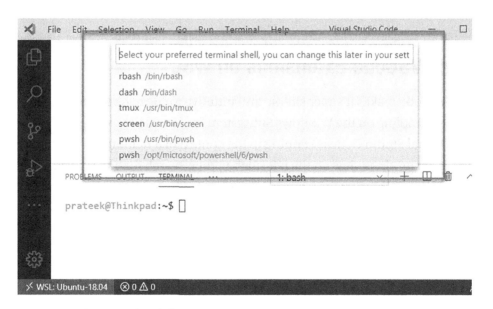

Figure 8-24. *Selecting the default shell for the VSCode terminal*

3.   Choose your favorite shell and kill the terminal by clicking the "bin" icon on the top-right corner of the terminal in Visual Studio Code.

4.   Figure 8-25 demonstrates that when you relaunch your terminal, it will open the default shell you selected in the previous step.

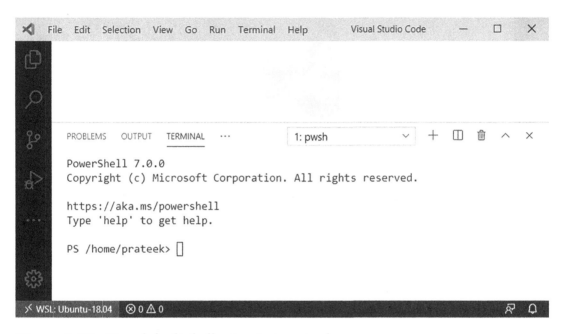

Figure 8-25. *New default shell setup in terminal*

Installing VSCode Extensions on WSL

Visual Studio Code makes it super simple and intuitive for developers to install extensions and tooling on the Windows Subsystem for Linux. For example, when an instance of Visual Studio Code is running in the context of a Remote - WSL instance, and if we click the Extensions view on the left sidebar, then search for an extension like in Figure 8-26.

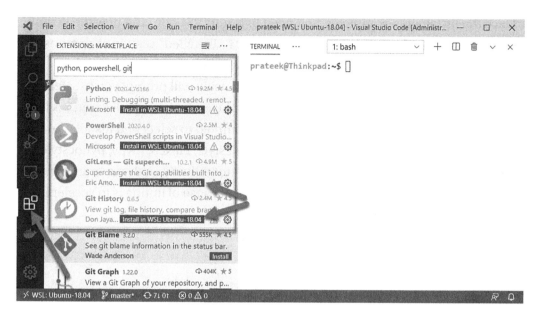

Figure 8-26. *Installing VSCode extensions in WSL*

As we can see, some of these extensions on Windows are compatible with WSL and show an "Install in WSL: <Distro Name>" button highlighted in green. If we click a button, it will install the extension on WSL. Let's install the Python extension just for sake of an example as demonstrated in Figure 8-27.

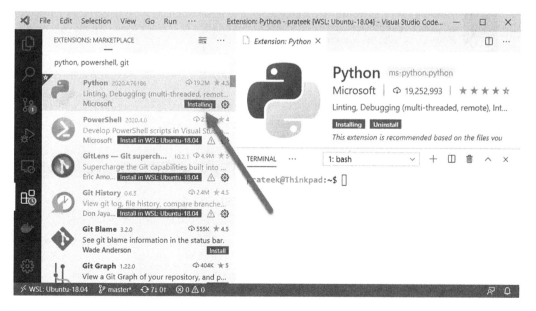

Figure 8-27. *Installation of VSCode extensions in progress on WSL*

Once the installation completes, you need to restart VSCode, and now the Python extension appears under the "WSL: UBUNTU-18.04 - Installed" section as demonstrated in Figure 8-28. If you are performing this setup for the first time, you will observe few other pop-ups on your screen, like VSCode extension will prompt you to select a Python interpreter; once the interpreter is chosen, the extension enables features like IntelliSense and debugging. You would be also prompted to select and install a linter, where various linters can be used like Pylint, pycodestyle, Flake8, mypy, pydocstyle, prospector, and pylama. Linting is a process that automatically analyzes your Python programs for errors and simplifies fixing them; the purpose of linting is to accelerate the development process and improve code quality.

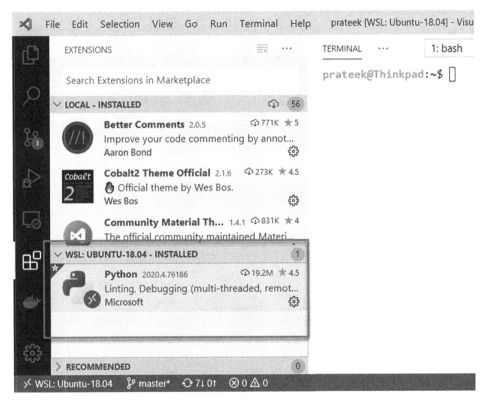

Figure 8-28. *VSCode extension installed on WSL*

Editing WSL Files and File Explorer

So now that we have the Python extension installed in WSL, we can run the following command in WSL's bash terminal to open a Python program from WSL in Visual Studio Code:

```
Code script.py
```

Additionally, a remote folder on WSL can be accessed within Visual Studio Code from the left sidebar by clicking the file explorer icon and then the "Open Folder" button as demonstrated in Figure 8-29.

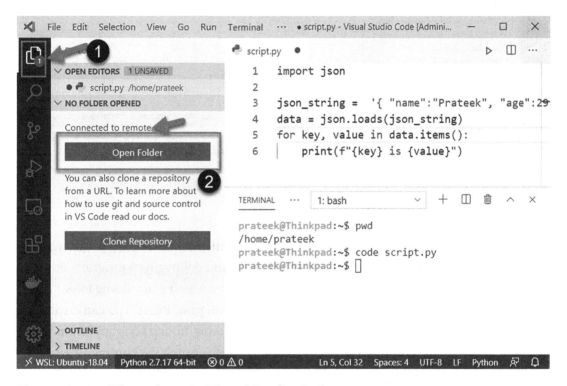

Figure 8-29.   *File explorer in Visual Studio Code*

As highlighted in Figure 8-30, this will give access to all the files in the directory and the ability to create files and folders in WSL using Visual Studio Code.

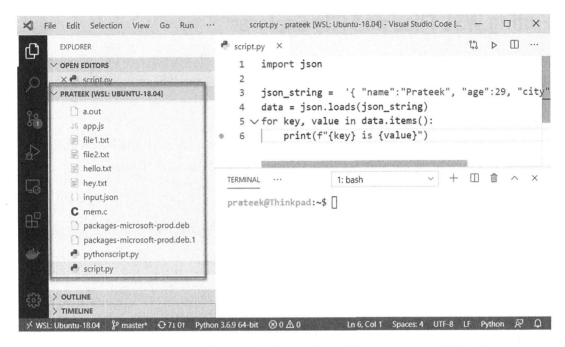

Figure 8-30. *Accessing WSL files and folders from file explorer in VSCode*

Running and Debugging Programs

Once we have the tooling set up and the ability to edit and create files and programs in WSL from Visual Studio Code, next comes running and debugging a program. For example, we have the following simple Python program created at my home folder /home/prateek to parse a JSON string and iterate over and print items. You can create a file named script.py at your current working directory using "touch script.py" from the terminal in WSL context and open this file in VSCode by running the command "code script.py" as shown as step 1 in Figure 8-31, then copy and paste the following code sample in the file, and finally save it by pressing Ctrl + S:

```
import json

json_string = '{ "name":"Prateek", "age":29, "city":"Bengaluru"}'

data = json.loads(json_string)
for key, value in data.items():
    print(f"{key} is {value}")
```

After creating the script.py file and opening it in Visual Studio Code, now we will set a breakpoint at line 7, by clicking in the far left margin next to a line of code in the editor window, which will set a red dot for a breakpoint as demonstrated in step 2 of Figure 8-31. Once that is done, click the "RUN" icon on the left sidebar highlighted as step 3 in Figure 8-31, which will open a debug console, then click the "Run and Debug" button in the debug console, and choose the debug configuration "Python File Debug the currently active Python file", which will run our program.

Figure 8-31. *Run and debug code on WSL in VSCode on Windows*

Since we have set up a breakpoint at line 7, the code execution pauses at that line and now you can see the value of runtime variables like "key" and "value" as highlighted in Figure 8-32, and we can keep stepping over these breakpoints by hitting F10 key, when the flow of control is in the "for" loop just to inspect how the values of runtime variables change as the program continues to execute. Additionally, we can also create watches and navigate the call stack of the program running on WSL from Windows.

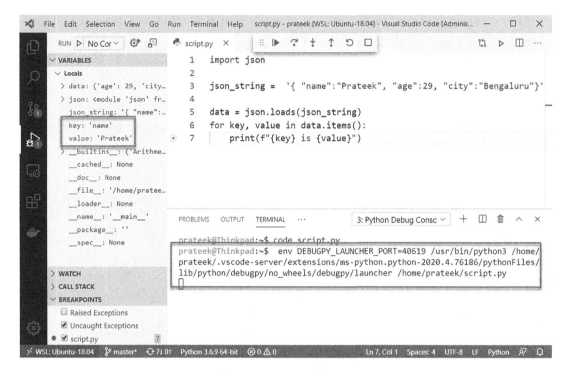

Figure 8-32. *Inspecting variables and values of Python program on WSL*

This debugging experience from a program running on WSL is made possible because of the VSCode Python extension that sets up a communication channel through the Visual Studio Code Server running on the Windows Subsystem for Linux.

Docker Containers on WSL2

The community version of Docker for Windows, also known as Docker Desktop, can download for Windows 10 64-bit Professional or Enterprise version from the Docker hub. Docker Desktop after recent architectural changes for Windows 10 now has the capacity to run with Windows Subsystem for Linux version 2 (WSL2) which is deployed with lightweight utility virtual machines (VMs). The new architecture works exactly like the Remote - WSL extension we discussed in the previous section. A server is set up on WSL2 to access and manage container life cycle from Windows 10. That means all Docker CLI commands executed on Windows 10 (host) machines are forwarded to WSL2 (VM) and run on the Docker integration package.

Download Docker Desktop from Docker Hub and follow the instructions on the official website for Docker to install it on Windows 10 machine; once the installation is complete, make sure to reboot the system for changes to take effect.

Download - `https://hub.docker.com/editions/community/docker-ce-desktop-windows/`

Installation - `https://docs.docker.com/docker-for-windows/install/`

Before we can use Docker Desktop with the Windows Subsystem for Linux, first we need to check the Linux distros that are running on WSL2 using "wsl --list –verbose" and let's make sure that at least one of your WSL Linux distributions is set to use version 2.

```
wsl --set-version <distro name> 2
```

Example:

```
wsl --set-version ubuntu-18.04 2
```

Once this prerequisite and Docker Desktop is installed on your Windows 10 machine, please follow these steps to set up WSL2 integration:

1. Go to Start menu and search "Docker", and click the "Docker Desktop" as shown in Figure 8-33.

Figure 8-33. *Launch Docker Desktop from Windows 10 Start menu*

2. This will start Docker Desktop in the background if it isn't already running, and now at the bottom-right corner of the taskbar, right-click the Docker tray icon, which will pop up a menu, and click "Settings" as highlighted in Figure 8-34.

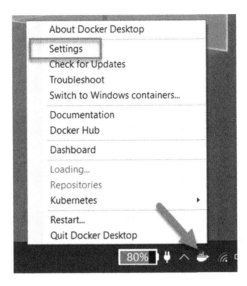

Figure 8-34. *Open Docker Settings*

3. Under the Settings window, go to "General", highlighted as step 1 in Figure 8-35, and check the box next to "Enable the experimental WSL2 based engine" which is step 2 in Figure 8-35.

Figure 8-35. *Enable WSL2 engine for Docker*

4. Now go to Settings ➤ Resources ➤ WSL Integration and enable all the WSL2 distribution packages you want to allow Docker containers to access.

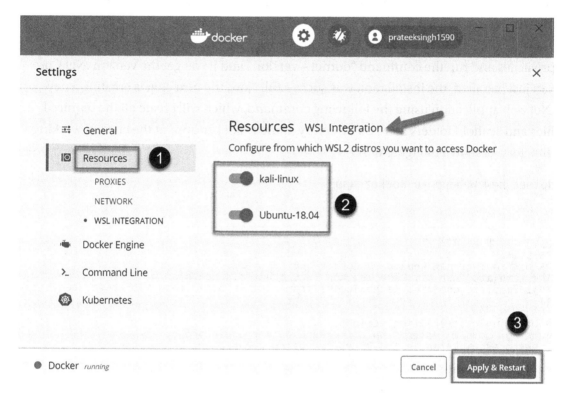

Figure 8-36. *Choose WSL distros to access Docker Desktop for Windows*

5. Finish the setup by clicking "Apply & Restart" as demonstrated in Figure 8-36.

Develop Web Application with Docker and WSL2

Once we have installed Docker Desktop and set it up to use WSL2 and Visual Studio Code is installed on your Windows machine, then developing with Docker on WSL2 is pretty straightforward and you can start working with your code inside the Linux distributions.

It is recommended to install the Docker extension from Microsoft on Visual Studio Code on both Windows 10 and WSL sides, so that you can see Docker containers, images, registries, networks, and volumes when connected to a WSL context using "Remote – WSL" extension and then you can even connect to interactive shells in the container.

Let's start with a simple ASP.Net Core web application, and then we will put web application code inside Docker containers; only prerequisite is to download and install .Net Core SDK from the official download page `https://dotnet.microsoft.com/download` and follow these instructions to complete the installation: `https://docs.microsoft.com/en-us/dotnet/core/install/sdk`.

After the installation is complete, open a PowerShell console with administrative privileges and run the command "dotnet --version", and if you get the version .Net Core you just installed, the installation was successful. Now, the next step is creating a new .Net web application using the following command, which will create all the required files and scaffold folders in a new directory named "docker-app" at the current working directory as shown in Figure 8-37:

```
dotnet new webapp -o docker-app
```

```
Administrator: Windows PowerShell
PS D:\>
PS D:\> dotnet new webapp -o docker-app
The template "ASP.NET Core Web App" was created successfully.
This template contains technologies from parties other than Microsoft, see https
s.

Processing post-creation actions...
Running 'dotnet restore' on docker-app\docker-app.csproj...
  Restore completed in 104.25 ms for D:\docker-app\docker-app.csproj.

Restore succeeded.

PS D:\> Get-ChildItem .\docker-app\


    Directory: D:\docker-app


Mode                 LastWriteTime         Length Name
----                 -------------         ------ ----
d-----         4/29/2020     3:57 PM                obj
d-----         4/29/2020     3:57 PM                Pages
d-----         4/29/2020     3:57 PM                Properties
d-----         4/29/2020     3:57 PM                wwwroot
-a----         4/29/2020     3:57 PM            162 appsettings.Development.json
-a----         4/29/2020     3:57 PM            192 appsettings.json
-a----         4/29/2020     3:57 PM            199 docker-app.csproj
-a----         4/29/2020     3:57 PM            718 Program.cs
-a----         4/29/2020     3:57 PM           1702 Startup.cs


PS D:\> _
```

Figure 8-37. *Create a simple .Net web application*

Now create a directory with the same name "docker-app" on WSL distro and copy all files/folders of ASP.Net Core application to your Linux distribution running on WSL2 as shown in Figure 8-38, under the new directory using the following PowerShell command:

```
Copy-Item D:\docker-app\* \\wsl$\Ubuntu-18.04\home\prateek\docker-app\
-Recurse
```

```
Administrator: Windows PowerShell
PS D:\>
PS D:\> Copy-Item D:\docker-app\* \\wsl$\Ubuntu-18.04\home\prateek\docker-app\ -Verbose
VERBOSE: Performing the operation "Copy Directory" on target "Item: D:\docker-app\obj Destination:
\\wsl$\Ubuntu-18.04\home\prateek\docker-app\obj".
VERBOSE: Performing the operation "Create Directory" on target "Destination: \\wsl$\Ubuntu-18.04\home\pr
VERBOSE: Performing the operation "Copy Directory" on target "Item: D:\docker-app\Pages Destination:
\\wsl$\Ubuntu-18.04\home\prateek\docker-app\Pages".
VERBOSE: Performing the operation "Create Directory" on target "Destination: \\wsl$\Ubuntu-18.04\home\pr
VERBOSE: Performing the operation "Copy Directory" on target "Item: D:\docker-app\Properties Destinatior
\\wsl$\Ubuntu-18.04\home\prateek\docker-app\Properties".
VERBOSE: Performing the operation "Create Directory" on target "Destination: \\wsl$\Ubuntu-18.04\home\pr
VERBOSE: Performing the operation "Copy Directory" on target "Item: D:\docker-app\wwwroot Destination:
\\wsl$\Ubuntu-18.04\home\prateek\docker-app\wwwroot".
VERBOSE: Performing the operation "Create Directory" on target "Destination: \\wsl$\Ubuntu-18.04\home\pr
VERBOSE: Performing the operation "Copy File" on target "Item: D:\docker-app\appsettings.Development.jsc
\\wsl$\Ubuntu-18.04\home\prateek\docker-app\appsettings.Development.json".
VERBOSE: Performing the operation "Copy File" on target "Item: D:\docker-app\appsettings.json Destinatic
\\wsl$\Ubuntu-18.04\home\prateek\docker-app\appsettings.json".
VERBOSE: Performing the operation "Copy File" on target "Item: D:\docker-app\docker-app.csproj Destinat
\\wsl$\Ubuntu-18.04\home\prateek\docker-app\docker-app.csproj".
VERBOSE: Performing the operation "Copy File" on target "Item: D:\docker-app\Program.cs Destination:
\\wsl$\Ubuntu-18.04\home\prateek\docker-app\Program.cs".
VERBOSE: Performing the operation "Copy File" on target "Item: D:\docker-app\Startup.cs Destination:
\\wsl$\Ubuntu-18.04\home\prateek\docker-app\Startup.cs".
PS D:\> _
```

Figure 8-38. *Copy .Net application files from Windows to WSL*

Once we have copied all the required files into WSL under the "docker-app" folder, we need to create a file named "Dockerfile" inside the "docker-app" folder with the following content. A Dockerfile is a simple text document with all the commands and instructions required in order to automatically build or assemble a container image:

```
FROM mcr.microsoft.com/dotnet/core/sdk:3.1 AS build-env
WORKDIR /app

# Copy csproj and restore as distinct layers
COPY *.csproj ./
RUN dotnet restore

# Copy everything else and build
COPY . ./
RUN dotnet publish -c Release -o out
```

```
# Build runtime image
FROM mcr.microsoft.com/dotnet/core/aspnet:3.1
WORKDIR /app

COPY --from=build-env /app/out .
ENTRYPOINT ["dotnet", "docker-app.dll"]
```

To limit the build context, create another file named ".dockerignore" to the "docker-app" directory with the following content:

```
/bin
/obj
```

Then we will do a little customization and edit our docker-app ➤ Pages ➤ index.cshtml file in our ASP.Net Core web application by modifying a heading <h1>..</h1> on the home page as highlighted in the text editor window of Figure 8-39 and then saving the changes.

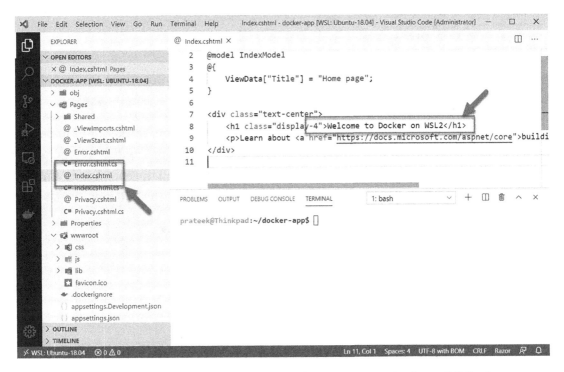

Figure 8-39. *Edit the ASP.Net Core web application on WSL from VSCode*

Once the Dockerfile and .dockerignore files are created and you are finished with you customizations, now it is time to build the Docker containers using the "docker build" command from bash shell in WSL, which will execute the instructions under Dockerfile and build the containers as shown in Figure 8-40.

```
docker build -t docker-app .
```

```
prateek@Thinkpad:~/docker-app$ docker build -t docker-app .
Sending build context to Docker daemon  4.403MB
Step 1/10 : FROM mcr.microsoft.com/dotnet/core/sdk:3.1 AS build-env
 ---> 4aa6a74611ff
Step 2/10 : WORKDIR /app
 ---> Using cache
 ---> d67edefe00de
Step 3/10 : COPY *.csproj ./
 ---> Using cache
 ---> ed7812bd7e29
Step 4/10 : RUN dotnet restore
 ---> Using cache
 ---> 4e4de39723e3
Step 5/10 : COPY . ./
 ---> Using cache
 ---> fabef529857e
Step 6/10 : RUN dotnet publish -c Release -o out
 ---> Using cache
 ---> b12a9dda00e6
Step 7/10 : FROM mcr.microsoft.com/dotnet/core/aspnet:3.1
 ---> 79e79777c3bf
Step 8/10 : WORKDIR /app
 ---> Using cache
 ---> 5610b276fab8
Step 9/10 : COPY --from=build-env /app/out .
 ---> Using cache
 ---> 5343bfe9ee01
Step 10/10 : ENTRYPOINT ["dotnet", "docker-app.dll"]
 ---> Using cache
 ---> 5aca11560f32
Successfully built 5aca11560f32
Successfully tagged docker-app:latest
prateek@Thinkpad:~/docker-app$
```

Figure 8-40. *Build docker image with ASP.Net Core web application*

Once the build is complete and you see success messages like the ones in Figure 8-40, we are good to run the Dockerized ASP.Net Core web application using the following command, which will run a container process and connect the ASP.Net Core web application listening on port 80 in docker container backed on WSL to localhost port 8080 of Windows 10 machine as shown in Figure 8-41:

```
docker run -d -p 8080:80 --name mywebapp docker-app
```

```
prateek@Thinkpad:~/docker-app$ docker run -d -p 8080:80 --name mywebapp docker-app
b4fb31cd53ee789cd26a4657b0b2323c5f4d7958354f0045239b582ea6a1ad94
prateek@Thinkpad:~/docker-app$ docker ps
CONTAINER ID        IMAGE               COMMAND               CREATED         STATUS
b4fb31cd53ee        docker-app          "dotnet docker-app.d..."  9 seconds ago   Up 8 seconds
prateek@Thinkpad:~/docker-app$ █
```

Figure 8-41. *Run docker container in WSL*

Now if you launch your web browser and navigate to http://localhost:8080, you can access your ASP.Net Core web application with the modifications we did on the index HTML page in one of the previous steps. This will run a web application hosted on docker container inside WSL2 backed as highlighted in Figure 8-42.

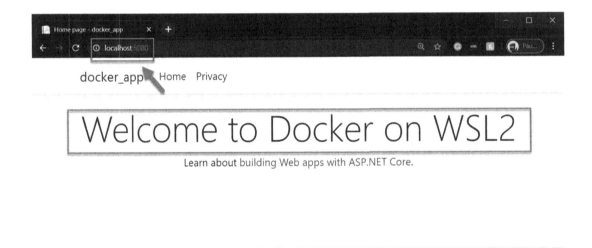

Figure 8-42. *Accessing dockerized ASP.Net Core web application*

If you have the Docker extension installed, then you can click the "Docker" icon on the left sidebar to open an Explorer window, where you can find the container and images which we just created and Docker registries and networking components. This extension gives you a graphical way to manage and inspect your Docker resources from the comfort in your Visual Studio Code IDE as demonstrated in Figure 8-43, where you develop the application that has been containerized in Docker.

Note   Please install the Docker extension from Visual Studio Marketplace using
the following link, or directly search it from the extensions on the left sidebar of
Visual Studio Code:

```
https://marketplace.visualstudio.com/items?itemName=ms-
azuretools.vscode-docker
```

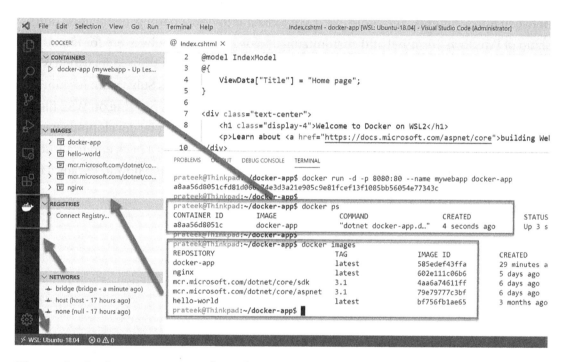

Figure 8-43. *Inspecting WSL-based Docker containers using Docker VSCode
extension*

Summary

In this chapter, we focused on development tools that can work with WSL and enhance the overall developer experience with WSL by providing a seamless Linux environment for developers to write code and develop applications with the minimum friction possible. We started the chapter by learning the version control tool Git and some caveats and workarounds that we need to perform to overcome text line-ending differences between the Windows and Linux environments, sharing credentials between environments, and more. Next, we looked into downloading, installation, and setup of Windows Terminal and customizing it to use Windows Subsystem for Linux distros. Later we learned to install, set up, and configure Visual Studio Code, which is a Microsoft open source, cross-platform editor, with the Windows Subsystem for Linux and also performed step-by-step debugging of a Python program residing on WSL file system from the Windows side. Finally, we concluded the chapter by developing an ASP.Net Core web application in a docker container with WSL2 as a back end in Visual Studio Code. In the next and final chapter, we will learn step by step how to deploy a full desktop experience on WSL.

CHAPTER 9

Linux Desktop on WSL

In this chapter, we are going to learn about the tools and services that are required to enable a desktop experience on the Windows Subsystem for Linux and a step-by-step configuration and setup process. To provide a full desktop experience on the Windows Subsystem for Linux, there are two important requirements. Firstly, we need a desktop environment that lets users interact with Linux with menus and multiple windowed applications using a graphical user interface. Secondly, we need a service that can connect the Windows user to the Linux desktop environment running on WSL.

We will learn how to use "Xfce" as the desktop environment and "xRDP" as a service to run a Remote Desktop Protocol (RDP) Server on a Linux distribution that can understand the incoming RDP connection requests from Windows.

Let's look into the steps involved in configuring a Linux desktop one by one.

Xfce

Xfce is a free and open source desktop environment for Unix-like operating systems, which is visually appealing and user-friendly compared to a command-line interface as shown in Figure 9-1. Xfce is very thin and lightweight, so it has a minimal resource (memory and CPU) footprint on the system.

Like the GNOME desktop, Xfce is also based on GTK, which is a popular toolkit for creating graphical user interface (GUI) programs that works with the X Window System. Toolkits like GTK enable developers to create windows, menus, and pop-up dialogs for interaction with users and other GUI programs.

Multiple packages and components come together to provide the full functionality of a desktop environment which is highly configurable, which means users can opt in or out from all available packages to build a desktop experience suitable to their own needs. Some of the core components of Xfce are these:

© Prateek Singh 2020
P. Singh, *Learn Windows Subsystem for Linux*, https://doi.org/10.1007/978-1-4842-6038-8_9

- **Window Manager** – Controls and manages the placement of windows on the screen

- **Desktop Manager** – Handles background image, menus, and the desktop

- **Panel** – Provides ability to switch between windows and applications

- **Session Manager** – Manages user login sessions

- **Application Finder** – Categorizes and displays installed applications so that they are easily accessible to the user

- **File Manager** – Provides file management capabilities in a graphical user interface

- **Setting Manager** – Controls all the settings of the desktop experience such as themes and display settings

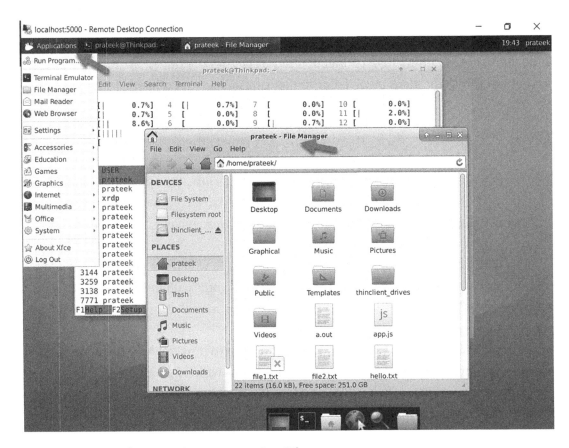

Figure 9-1. *Desktop environment using Xfce*

xRDP

xRDP is an open source tool which allows Windows users to access the Linux desktop remotely through Windows Remote Desktop Protocol (RDP) by providing a graphical interface to log in and connect to the remote machine. Supported RDP clients (such as MSTSC.exe) can send connection requests to the xRDP server running on the Linux distribution. Some of the supported RDP clients are

- Microsoft Terminal Services Client (MSTSC)

- FreeRDP

- Rdesktop

- NeutrinoRDP

In other words, xRDP is an open source implementation of the proprietary Microsoft RDP protocol that can bridge connectivity for Windows users to a Linux system over a network connection. xRDP now supports Transport Layer Security (TLS) protocol, which makes it more secure.

All xRDP configuration settings are stored in the file /etc/xrdp/xrdp.ini where you can find settings like the port number on which users can connect to the Linux desktop or the protocol settings used to secure the connection, like RDP, TLS, or Negotiate as shown in Figure 9-2.

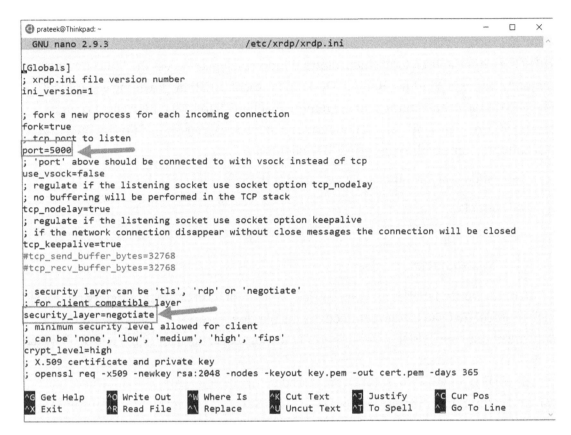

Figure 9-2. *xRDP server configuration through the /etc/xrdp/xrdp.ini config file*

The xRDP server also maintains a log of all the incoming connections port binding, enabling a security layer, and so on in the log file /var/log/xrdp.log as demonstrated in Figure 9-3.

```
prateek@Thinkpad: ~                                              —    □    ×
prateek@Thinkpad:~$ sudo service xrdp start
 * Starting Remote Desktop Protocol server
[20200418-23:00:16] [DEBUG] Testing if xrdp can listen on 0.0.0.0 port 5000.
[20200418-23:00:16] [DEBUG] Closed socket 6 (AF_INET6 :: port 5000)
                                                                  [ OK ]
prateek@Thinkpad:~$ cat /var/log/xrdp.log
[20200418-23:00:16] [DEBUG] Testing if xrdp can listen on 0.0.0.0 port 5000.
[20200418-23:00:16] [DEBUG] Closed socket 6 (AF_INET6 :: port 5000)
[20200418-23:00:18] [INFO ] starting xrdp with pid 976
[20200418-23:00:18] [INFO ] listening to port 5000 on 0.0.0.0
[20200418-23:01:09] [INFO ] Socket 11: AF_INET6 connection received from ::1 port 55537
[20200418-23:01:09] [DEBUG] Closed socket 11 (AF_INET6 ::1 port 5000)
[20200418-23:01:09] [DEBUG] Closed socket 10 (AF_INET6 :: port 5000)
[20200418-23:01:09] [INFO ] Using default X.509 certificate: /etc/xrdp/cert.pem
[20200418-23:01:09] [INFO ] Using default X.509 key file: /etc/xrdp/key.pem
[20200418-23:01:09] [ERROR] Cannot read private key file /etc/xrdp/key.pem: Permission denied
[20200418-23:01:09] [DEBUG] TLSv1.2 enabled
[20200418-23:01:09] [DEBUG] TLSv1.1 enabled
[20200418-23:01:09] [DEBUG] TLSv1 enabled
[20200418-23:01:09] [DEBUG] Security layer: requested 11, selected 0
[20200418-23:01:09] [DEBUG] Closed socket 11 (AF_INET6 ::1 port 5000)
[20200418-23:01:09] [INFO ] Socket 11: AF_INET6 connection received from ::1 port 55538
[20200418-23:01:09] [DEBUG] Closed socket 11 (AF_INET6 ::1 port 5000)
[20200418-23:01:09] [DEBUG] Closed socket 10 (AF_INET6 :: port 5000)
[20200418-23:01:09] [INFO ] Using default X.509 certificate: /etc/xrdp/cert.pem
[20200418-23:01:09] [INFO ] Using default X.509 key file: /etc/xrdp/key.pem
[20200418-23:01:09] [ERROR] Cannot read private key file /etc/xrdp/key.pem: Permission denied
[20200418-23:01:09] [DEBUG] TLSv1.2 enabled
[20200418-23:01:09] [DEBUG] TLSv1.1 enabled
```

Figure 9-3. *xRDP server logs stored in /var/log/xrdp.log*

Now that we understand what Xfce and xRDP do, let's set up a desktop environment on the Windows Subsystem for Linux, which will provide a full graphical user interface (GUI) and enhance the overall development experience.

Note   We have been using the Ubuntu 18.04 distributions in all the examples of the book, but since April 2020, Ubuntu 20.04 LTS Linux distribution has been released for WSL, so we will base all our examples in this last chapter on the latest release of Ubuntu. Before we can proceed with the examples, please go to the Microsoft Store and download the "Ubuntu 20.04 LTS" Linux distribution package on your machine.

Setup and Configuration

In order to achieve the desktop experience on the Windows Subsystem for Linux

1. Open the Ubuntu 20.04 LTS distribution on the Windows Subsystem for Linux, and fully update the distro by running the following command. This step may take some time to finish updating, depending upon your Internet speed, so please allow it to complete as shown in Figure 9-4.

```
sudo apt update && sudo apt upgrade -y
```

```
prateek@Thinkpad: ~
prateek@Thinkpad:~$
prateek@Thinkpad:~$ sudo apt update && sudo apt upgrade -y
Hit:1 http://archive.ubuntu.com/ubuntu bionic InRelease
Get:2 http://security.ubuntu.com/ubuntu bionic-security InRelease [88.7 kB]
Get:3 http://archive.ubuntu.com/ubuntu bionic-updates InRelease [88.7 kB]
Hit:4 https://packages.microsoft.com/ubuntu/18.04/prod bionic InRelease
Get:5 http://archive.ubuntu.com/ubuntu bionic-backports InRelease [74.6 kB]
Fetched 252 kB in 2s (161 kB/s)
Reading package lists... Done
Building dependency tree
Reading state information... Done
All packages are up to date.
Reading package lists... Done
Building dependency tree
Reading state information... Done
Calculating upgrade... Done
The following package was automatically installed and is no longer required:
  libdumbnet1
Use 'sudo apt autoremove' to remove it.
0 upgraded, 0 newly installed, 0 to remove and 0 not upgraded.
1 not fully installed or removed.
After this operation, 0 B of additional disk space will be used.
Setting up blueman (2.0.5-1ubuntu1) ...
```

Figure 9-4. *Update and upgrade a Linux distro*

2. Once the preceding step is complete, install both the Xfce and xRDP servers using the following commands. If this triggers a Windows Defender Firewall warning, then please go ahead and click "Allow access" for the private networks.

```
sudo apt install xfce4 xrdp
```

3. Once the installation from the previous step is complete, we need to make sure xRDP is not using port 3389 as shown in Figure 9-5, or it will conflict with any RDP server that might be running on the Windows host.

```
prateek@Thinkpad: ~
prateek@Thinkpad:~$
prateek@Thinkpad:~$ cat /etc/xrdp/xrdp.ini
[Globals]
; xrdp.ini file version number
ini_version=1

; fork a new process for each incoming connection
fork=true
; tcp port to listen
port=3389  ◄───────
; 'port' above should be connected to with vsock instead of tcp
use_vsock=false
; regulate if the listening socket use socket option tcp_nodelay
; no buffering will be performed in the TCP stack
tcp_nodelay=true
; regulate if the listening socket use socket option keepalive
; if the network connection disappear without close messages the conne(
tcp_keepalive=true
#tcp_send_buffer_bytes=32768
#tcp_recv_buffer_bytes=32768
```

Figure 9-5. *By default, the xRDP server listens on RDP port 3389*

4. Change the settings in /etc/xrdp/xrdp.ini so that the xRDP server listens on port 5000 for Ubuntu 18.04 running over WSL using any text editor (e.g., nano), and it should look like Figure 9-6.

```
sudo nano /etc/xrdp/xrdp.ini
```

```
prateek@Thinkpad: ~
prateek@Thinkpad:~$
prateek@Thinkpad:~$ cat /etc/xrdp/xrdp.ini
[Globals]
; xrdp.ini file version number
ini_version=1

; fork a new process for each incoming connection
fork=true
; tcp port to listen
port=5000  ⟵
; 'port' above should be connected to with vsock instead of tcp
use_vsock=false
; regulate if the listening socket use socket option tcp_nodelay
; no buffering will be performed in the TCP stack
tcp_nodelay=true
; regulate if the listening socket use socket option keepalive
; if the network connection disappear without close messages the con
```

Figure 9-6. *Configure the xRDP server to listen on port 5000*

5. Start the xRDP service on the Linux distribution using the following
command, and as shown in Figure 9-7, you will see that the Remote
Desktop Protocol Server will begin listening on the designated port,
which will be used by Microsoft RDP client (mstsc.exe) to connect
to Ubuntu 18.04 and provide a full desktop experience.

```
sudo service xrdp start
```

It is required to run "xrdp" service every time you want to establish a remote
session, but you can also create a startup script to run this every time you start the Linux
distribution, which will make sure the service is running when you want it.

```
prateek@Thinkpad: ~                                          —    □    ×
prateek@Thinkpad:~$
prateek@Thinkpad:~$ sudo service xrdp start
[sudo] password for prateek:
 * Starting Remote Desktop Protocol server
[20200418-17:33:36] [DEBUG] Testing if xrdp can listen on 0.0.0.0 port 5000.
[20200418-17:33:36] [DEBUG] Closed socket 6 (AF_INET6 :: port 5000)
                                                            [ OK ]
prateek@Thinkpad:~$
```

Figure 9-7. *Start xRDP service*

6. If the previous step was successful without any errors as demonstrated in Figure 9-7, then you are pretty much done with the setup and configuration.

7. Now, launch the Windows Remote Desktop Connection Manager (mstsc.exe) and connect to "localhost" on port 5000 as shown in Figure 9-8. Please note that this only works for WSL1, and since WSL2 runs on lightweight utility VM with a dedicated network interface, you may need to obtain the IP address in order to establish a remote desktop connection to a WSL2 instance.

Figure 9-8. *Connect xRDP server using a remote desktop client*

8. If the preceding step fails, launch a PowerShell console with administrative privileges and run the following command that will restart the Linux instance, and then launch the WSL again. Now, start the "xrdp" service as mentioned in step 5 and try step 7 again.

```
Get-Service LxssManager | Restart-Service
```

9. This will establish an RDP connection to the Linux distro running on WSL, which we just configured with Xfce and xRDP.

10. Now simply supply the user credentials for Ubuntu 18.04 and hit OK button as shown in the Figure 9-9.

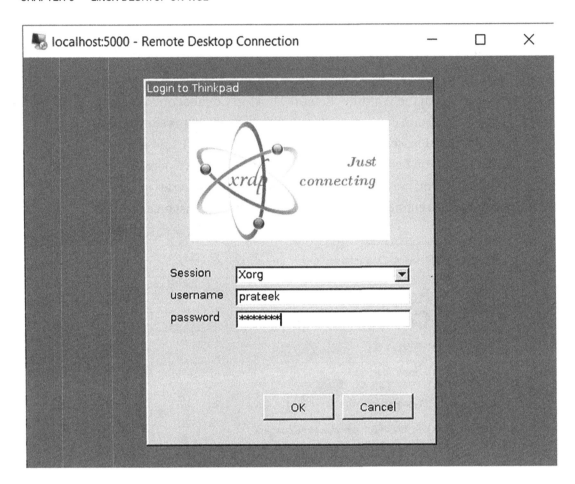

Figure 9-9. *Provide Linux credentials*

11.   Once the credentials are provided xRDP will launch a full desktop
experience as shown in Figure 9-10 running on WSL.

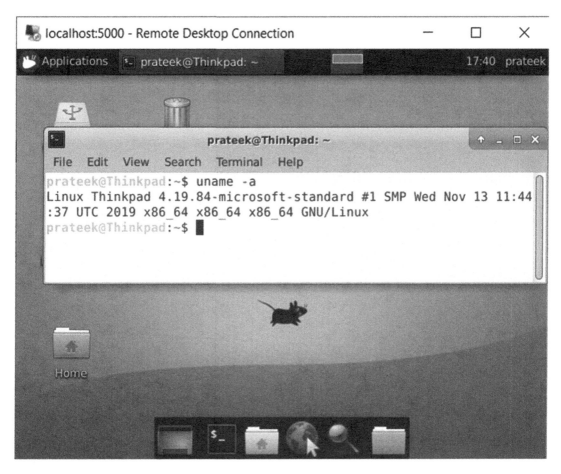

Figure 9-10. *Linux desktop on the Windows Subsystem for Linux*

Summary

In this chapter, we learned step-by-step installation and configuration of Xfce and xRDP that enable a full desktop experience on the Windows Subsystem for Linux. Once the setup is complete, it lets users interact with the Windows Subsystem for Linux instance using a graphical user interface. Xfce creates a desktop environment for the users, and xRDP is the service that allows Windows users to connect to Linux instances through the RDP protocol.

Index

© Prateek Singh 2020
P. Singh, *Learn Windows Subsystem for Linux*, https://doi.org/10.1007/978-1-4842-6038-8

X, Y, Z

Printed in the United States
By Bookmasters